The Complete Instant Pot Duo Crisp Air Fryer Cookbook

Mouthwatering, Healthy and Quick-to-Make Recipes for Smart People to Roast, Bake, Broil and Dehydrate

By Dr James Goodman

Copyright © 2020 Dr James Goodman

All rights reserved. No part of this guide may be reproduced in any form without permission in writing from the publisher except in the case of brief quotations embodied in critical articles or reviews.

Legal & Disclaimer

The information contained in this book and its contents is not designed to replace or take the place of any form of medical or professional advice; and is not meant to replace the need for independent medical, financial, legal or other professional advice or services, as may be required. The content and information in this book has been provided for educational and entertainment purposes only.

The content and information contained in this book has been compiled from sources deemed reliable, and it is accurate to the best of the Author's knowledge, information and belief. However, the Author cannot guarantee its accuracy and validity and cannot be held liable for any errors and/or omissions. Further, changes are periodically made to this book as and when needed. Where appropriate and/or necessary, you must consult a professional (including but not limited to your doctor, attorney, financial advisor or such other professional advisor) before using any of the suggested remedies, techniques, or information in this book.

Upon using the contents and information contained in this book, you agree to hold harmless the Author from and against any damages, costs, and expenses, including any legal fees potentially resulting from the application of any of the information provided by this book. This disclaimer applies to any loss, damages or injury caused by the use and application, whether directly or indirectly, of any advice or information presented, whether for breach of contract, tort, negligence, personal injury, criminal intent, or under any other cause of action.

You agree to accept all risks of using the information presented inside this book.

You agree that by continuing to read this book, where appropriate and/or necessary, you shall consult a professional (including but not limited to your doctor, attorney, or financial advisor or such other advisor as needed) before using any of the suggested remedies, techniques, or information in this book.

Table of Content

Introduction 1
Chapter 1 Understanding the New Appliance Duo Crisp Air Fryer 2
    What is Instant Pot Duo Crisp Air Fryer? 2
    Control Panel of Instant Pot Duo Crisp Air Fryer 3
    Benefits of Instant Pot Duo Crisp Air Fryer: It Comes with Two Multiple Function Lids 3
    Things Worth Knowing Before Purchasing Instant Pot Duo Crisp Air Fryer 4
    Other Things to Consider 5
    Features and Specifications 5
    Important Reminders and Safety Tips 5
    What Error Code Means 6
    Troubleshooting 7
    FAQ about the Duo Crisp Air Fryer 9
Chapter 2 Breakfast and Lunch 10
    Air-fried Scotch Eggs 10
    Simple & Easy Mac and Cheese 11
    Instant Pot Pepperoni Pasta 12
    Big Bite Sandwich 13
    Cheesy Air Fryer Spaghetti 14
    Healthy Breakfast Bake 15
    Perfect Bacon & Croissant Breakfast 16
    Air-fried French Toast Sticks 17
    Ranchero Brunch Crunch Wraps 18
    Crunchy Breakfast Nuggets 19
    Air Fryer Garlic Bread 20
Chapter 3 Vegan and Vegetarian 21
    Crispy Air-Fried Brussels Sprouts 21
    Air-fried Green Beans 22
    Roasted Asparagus 23
    Air Fryer Crispy Broccoli 24
    Air Fried Acorn Squash 25
    Air-fried Avocado 26
    Mediterranean Veggies 27

 Rosemary Air-fried Potatoes 28

 Air Fryer Falafel Balls 29

 Air Fried Cauliflower Rice 30

Chapter 4 Fish and Seafood 31

 Crisp-fried Salmon 31

 Air Fryer Tuna Patties 32

 Air Fryer Garlic-lemon Shrimp 33

 Air Fried White Fish with Garlic & Lemon 34

 Air-fried Shrimps with Lemon 35

 Air-fried Crumbed Fish 36

 Air Fryer Coconut Shrimp 37

 Air Fryer Fish Sticks 38

 Air Fryer Lobster Tails with Lemon-garlic Butter 39

 Air Fried Shrimps 40

 Crisp Shrimp ala Bang Bang 41

 Air-fryer Cajun Salmon 42

Chapter 5 Beef, Lamb, and Pork 43

 Air Fryer Steak 43

 Italian-style Air-fried Meatballs 44

 Air Fryer Pork Chops 45

 Air Fryer Bacon Recipe 46

 Air Fryer Pork Chop Bites with Mushrooms 47

 Air Fryer Pork Belly Bites 48

 Air Fryer Steak Bites & Mushrooms 49

 Air Fryer Steak Tips 50

 Air-fried Garlic-rosemary Lamb Chops 51

 Air Fryer Sweet and Sour Pork 52

 Baby Back Ribs 53

 Pork Meatballs 54

Chapter 6 Poultry 55

 Instant Pot Turkey Breast 55

 Instant Pot Rotisserie Chicken 56

 Asian Sticky Wings 57

 Crisp Greek Chicken & Potatoes 58

 Chicken Fillet 59

 Honey-mustard Chicken Breasts 60

Chicken-Parmesan Wings 61

Chicken Tikka Kebab 62

Super Crispy Chicken Wings 63

Mini Egg Bake 64

Cheesy Frittata 65

Southern-style Chicken 66

Air-fried Breaded Chicken 67

Crispy Chicken-vegetable Rolls 68

Air Fryer Bacon Wrapped Hot Dogs 69

Fryer Chicken Wings 70

Air Fryer Baked Egg Cups Spinach & Cheese 71

Chapter 7 Desserts 72

Air Fryer Brownies 72

Air-Fried Cinnamon Rolls 73

Chocolate Smarties Cookies 74

Lava Molten Cake 75

Air-fried Donuts 76

Key Lime Cheesecake 77

Chocolate Chip Cookie 78

Air Fried Chocolate Chips 79

Chapter 8 Snacks 80

Air Fried Cheeseburgers 80

Air-fried Pickles 81

Crispy Potatoes 82

Crispy Avocado Fries 83

Air Fryer Zucchini Chips 84

Air Fryer Sweet Potato French Fries 85

Air-fried Kale Chips 86

Air-fried Toasted Sticks 87

Air Fryer Banana Bread 88

Brussels Sprout Pizza 89

Introduction

Before the invention of Instant Pot, kitchen tasks can be demanding and rigorous especially for moms and those who have little time to spend cooking and preparing meals. However, with the advent of Instant Pot Multifunctional cooker, things become easier, yet there is still something that it failed to do among the many cooking tasks. For example, you can't expect to produce crispy air fried dishes with your Instant Pot. So having an air fryer is indeed a necessity for those who love fried and still want to stay healthy. Now, with this in mind, Instant Pot added a new item to their selection of innovative multi-cookers – the **Instant Pot Duo Crisp Air Fryer**.

Chapter 1 Understanding the New Appliance Duo Crisp Air Fryer

What is Instant Pot Duo Crisp Air Fryer?

Instant Pot has taken another obvious leap with their new Instant Pot Duo Crisp Air Fryer. Instant Pot is known for its obvious benefits of cooking meals in a fraction of time compared to the usual time it takes. Other than this, it also kills harmful bacteria, helps you save energy, and preserves the taste of food. If you are not armed with the best culinary skill, expect Instant Pot to save you when you need it.

Normally, Instant Pot can help you with 10 multi-cooking tasks:
- Sauté
- Pressure Cooker
- Rice Cooker
- Slow Cooker
- Food Warmer
- Cake Maker
- Yogurt Maker
- Searing
- Steamer
- Sterilizer

Now, Instant Pot has added one more special feature making it an 11-in-1 multifunctional pressure cooker. With its Duo Crisp Air Fryer model, it bears all the features of the Instant Multifunctional pressure cooker, but this time with two lids for attachments – the pressure cooker lid and the new innovative feature - the air fryer lid. With this added innovation, you will surely enjoy a new cooking experience with Instant Pot Duo Crisp Air Fryer.

With almost everything done with the touch of your fingertip, you will no longer be a slave to your kitchen and cooking tasks as well as clean-up task will no longer be as tiresome as they used to be for any housewife or cook.

Control Panel of Instant Pot Duo Crisp Air Fryer

The Instant Pot Crispy Air Fryer Lid is an attachment to the Instant Pot Duo Crisp Pressure Cooker. Simply put, the new Instant Pot Duo Crisp Air Fryer combines air frying with the rest of cooking features with just a swapping of lids. While the pressure cooker lid offers the following functions:

- Pressure Cook
- Sauté
- Slow Cook
- Sous Vide
- Keep Warm

On the other hand, the instant pot duo crisp air fryer lid offers the following:

- Air fry
- Roast
- Bake
- Broil
- Dehydrate

With its built-in smart programs, Instant Pot makes it easy for everyone to enjoy cooking whether they are chef or novice. Everyone can prepare their favorite healthy meal quick and fast.

Benefits of Instant Pot Duo Crisp Air Fryer: It Comes with Two Multiple Function Lids

When you purchase the Instant Pot Duo Crisp Air Fryer, you will be surprised to see that it comes with two completely separate lids. These two lids are both removable, which means that you can use them both one at a time depending on your cooking need. It's either you use the air pressure function or the air fryer function.

It's Available in 8-Quarts Size for Easy Frying

Although Instant Pot offers pressure and multi-cookers in 6-quarts and 8 quarts, the Air Fryer Lid is only available for 8-quarts size of Instant Pot

Safe and Easy Storage

The pressure cooker lid is equipped with a quick-release switch, which automatically resets to the default Sealed position once the lid is closed. Because it is connected to the base once installed, there is no need for a power cord in the Air Fryer Lid, which could be a potential source for accidents.

The air fryer lid also comes with a tray where you can safely place the lid while it is still hot. Just make sure that the Instant Pot logo is facing up when you do this. After the lid has cooled off, you may turn the tray over to attach the air frying lid in place for storing it safely.

Essential Smart Programs

Unlike other Instant Pot models for Pressure and multi-cookers, the Instant Pot Duo Crisp

Air Fryer includes only the basic essential buttons which make it more easy and convenient to use. Buttons for the Air Fryer features are already included in the control panel of the Instant Pot unit.

Comes with Accessories Designed for Convenience

Each of the accessories that come along with the Instant Pot Duo Crisp Air Fryer is designed for need and convenience.

The conventional trivet which usually comes with any Instant Pot model is now updated to include a handle that swings around to the other side and convertible to a tall rack that you may use to rest food.

The model also has a double-layered air fryer basket with legs that you can slide off for easy cleaning, and the stainless steel insert comes with two large holes to help you easily remove it from the pot.

Instant Pot Duo Crisp Air Fryer inner pot works incompatible with all oven-safe cookware.

However, before buying the Instant Pot Duo Crisp Air Fryer, there are things you need to consider.

Things Worth Knowing Before Purchasing Instant Pot Duo Crisp Air Fryer

The Start Button is Not Too Visible

This time, Instant Pot redesigned their button on the Duo Crisp using the GREEN button for the START and RED button to CANCEL. If you're not used to it, green is a bit hard to read compared to the rest of the buttons, but once you get used to it, things get easier.

Smaller Display

This time, the display buttons are also smaller compared to other Instant Pot models, which means smaller fonts that lessen visibility won't be a problem once you get used to it.

It Comes Only With a Starter Guide

The Instant Pot Duo Crisp only comes with a Getting Started Guide. If you want to read the complete manufacturer's manual for complete instructions on the product, you have to access their website as it is only available online.

The Air Fryer Lid is Exclusive to Instant Pot Duo Crisp

Unlike the Mealthy CrispLid - a competitor of Instant Pot, the Instant Pot Air Fryer Lid can't be used with other pressure cooker or multi-cookers or even to other Instant Pot pressure/multicookers models, but is exclusive only to Instant Pot Duo Crisp Air Fryer.

Not Enough Available Information on Air Frying

Unluckily, Instant Pot does not provide users with enough information about the Air Fryer Lid. Even their manual which is available online has very little to say about air frying but includes detailed charts for sous vide and pressure cooking. There are also no available recipes included, which could be a downside for the product.

Other Things to Consider

- In contrast to other Instant Pot models, the timer counts down the remaining cooking time in seconds for the remaining minute left.
- The Air Fryer starts alerting you with a beep after 5 minutes, 20 minutes, and 60 minutes after it starts cooking to let you know how soon it can be completed.
- Take note that the **KEEP WARM** and **DELAY START** functions do not work when you're using the Air Fryer Lid.
- The timer counts down in seconds after the remaining 1 minute unlike in other models of the Instant Pot.

- When you're using the Air Fryer Lid, be reminded that the Keep Warm and Delay Start do not function.

Features and Specifications

The size of the Instant Pot Duo Crisp 8-Quarts which is equivalent to its volume capacity and weighing 10.3 kilograms or 22.7 pounds.

The Instant Pot Duo Crisp Air Fryer is a bit over 22 pounds and requires 1500 watts. It uses a sensor to switch between 10.2 – 11.6psi on high pressure and between 5.8-7.2psi on the low-pressure setting.

The Instant Pot Duo Crisp is 14.8 inches (length) x 13.6 inches (width) x 14.2 inches (height) with the pressure cooker lid. When the Air Fryer Lid is attached, it measures 14.8 inches (length) x 13.6 inches (width) x 15.3 inches (height).

The Instant Pot Duo Crisp Air Fryer comes with the following:
- The external housing unit with an attached electrical cord
- The pressure cooker lid
- Sealing gasket for the pressure cooker
- Stainless steel trivet (rack)
- Two-level air fryer basket
- Removable stainless steel tray.

Important Reminders and Safety Tips

Turning Off the Sound

After turning on the Duo Crisp, press long the Time + Button and the display will show you if the sound is ON or OFF. Note, however, while the cooking function is at work, you can't turn off the sound and error alert will still sound off.

Safety Measures

Instant Pot was designed to get rid of some errors that usually cause harm or food spoilage in cooking. Having passed the stringent UL and ILC certification, Instant Pot assured you of an uncompromised safety when it comes to your cooking needs. It protects you through its 10 mechanisms that have been proven to be safe and are patented technologies.

Steam Release - Excess pressure is released by venting steam via the steam release handle/ valve

Anti-Block Shield - The lid of the pressure cooker automatically locks itself to prevent the opening of the cooker.

Lid Position Detection - The Instant Pot cooker will not allow cooking to start unless the lid is in a safe position.

Automatic Temperature Control - Based on the program, the heating is being regulated for pressure cooking to make sure that it remains within a safe temperature range.

Burn (Overheat) Protection - Overheating may occur when:
- The inner pot is not properly installed in place and the inner pot is not completely connected to the heating element
- When there is a heat distribution issue in the inner pot such as when residues accumulate at the bottom of the inner pot.
- After sautéing, food had stuck to the bottom of the inner pot and the pot has not been deglazed.

The cooker reduces the risk of burning by automatically lowering the heat output.

Automatic Pressure Control - It maintains functioning pressure levels and suspending heat in case pressure exceeds the required pressure level.

Electrical Fuse - If the electrical current exceeds safety limits, it will automatically cut off power.

Thermal Fuse - If the temperature inside the pot exceeds safety limits, the power will automatically cut off.

Leaky Lid Detection - In case of steam leakage from the lid such as when sealing is not installed or when the steam release handle is set on venting and not on sealing, the cooker automatically ceases to pressurize. The cooker monitors the preheating time and decreases heat output if within 40 minutes it has not reached the working pressure as loss of stem may cause to burn food.

What Error Code Means

Burn/Food Burn

When this burn notice is displayed, this means that the Instant Pot could be experiencing any of the following:
- The inner pot is not properly positions.
- The temperature in the cooking pot is too high.
- There is not enough liquid left on the inner pot.

- Some residues like starch could have deposited at the bottom of the cooking pot preventing heat from properly circulating.

Once you have this burn notification, immediately remove the inner pot from the Instant Pot base. If there are burn residues at the bottom of the pot, soak and scrub to remove.

When using the pot, make sure to use enough water and as much as possible, avoid ingredients containing thickening agents like prepackaged spaghetti sauce.

C5 – This indicates that the inner pot is not properly set up to the base or that there is not enough amount of water left.

C7 (NoPr) – This indicates that the heating element has failed. It could be that the quick-release switch is set to vent position or there is not enough liquid. If the error remains even after you have a check on the vent, release the valve, and make sure that you maintain the minimum liquid requirement for pressure, contact support immediately.

C9 – This indicates that the air fryer is not well connected to the unit base. Try pressing down the area right above the connector.

Lid – This indicates that could have used the wrong lid or the lid could have been wrongly positioned. Try to double-check the lid and make sure that you don't use the lid when using the sauté function.

PrSE – This indicates that while in a non-pressure cooking program, pressure has accumulated. Therefore, use the quick-release vent to lower the pressure inside the pot.

C1, C2, C6, C6H, and C6L: There is no specific instruction as to what these errors indicate although the Instant Pot is able to sense that something is wrong with the unit. Immediately contact support at 1-800-828-7280 or send an email to support@instantpot.com.

Troubleshooting

When there is occasional light cracking sound or ticking in your cooker, the one possible reason could be the sound of power switching and expanding pressure board during the change in temperature. This is normal and therefore needs no action to be taken.

Another **possible reason** could be the **wetness of the bottom part of the inner pot**. The solution is to wipe it dry and ensure that the heating element is dry before using it for cooking.

When the display remains blank even after the power cord is connected, then the possible reason could be a bad power connection or no power at all. The solution for this is to inspect the power cord and ensure that the detachable power cord is tightly plugged into the base power socket. You may likewise check other appliances on the same outlet.

The other possible reason could be that the cooker's electrical fuse has blown out, the immediately contact support.

1. When there's difficulty closing the Lid?

Reason #1: The sealing ring is not properly installed

Solution: Try repositioning the sealing ring and make sure it is snug behind the sealing ring rack.

Reason #2: Float valve could have popped up

Solution: Just press the valve downward gently with a long utensil

Reason #3: Cooker contents are still hot enough to produce steam

Solution: Turn into venting position the steam release handle and slowly lower the lid onto the cooker base to release heat.

2. When there's difficulty opening the lid?

Reason #1: Could be due to the pressure inside the cooker

Solution: Release pressure as required in the recipe and open lid only after it has depressurized and the float valve had dropped down

Reason #2: Float valve is stuck up in the popped-up position due to the presence of some residue

Solution #1: Make sure that the steam is completely released by the quick-release method before pressing the float valve gently using a long utensil.

Solution #2: Open lid with caution and thoroughly clean lid, float valve, and surrounding areas before using it again for your cooking need.

3. When steam leaks from the side of the lid?

Reason #1: Absence of sealing ring

Solution: Put the sealing ring

Reason #2: The sealing ring is either damaged or has worn out

Solution: Replace the sealing ring

Reason #3: There are food residues attached to the sealing ring

Solution: Remove and thoroughly clean it

Reason #4: Lid bot properly sealed or closed

Solution: Try opening and then closing the lid again

Reason #5: the Sealing ring is off-center

Solution: Remove the sealing ring and check for bends or warps. Contact customer service

Reason #6: Misshaped inner pot rim

Solution: Check for any deformation of inner pot rim and contact customer service.

FAQ about the Duo Crisp Air Fryer

1. What is the inner pot made of?

It is primarily made from 304 (18/8) stainless steel with the aluminum core at the 3-ply bottom for optimal use but ensures you that no aluminum comes in contact with the food you're cooking. There is also no aluminum coating and so the inner pot is in compliant with the FDA for safety standard requirements.

The steam rack is likewise made from food grade 304 (18/8) stainless steel, also ensuring safety for the food you're cooking.

The air fryer comes with a ceramic nonstick coating, making food easy to remove and the air fryer basket easy to clean.

2. Can the setting be adjusted when you have started cooking?

Even when you have started cooking, you can still make some adjustments to the cooking time, cooking temperature, and pressure level.

3. How many appliances can the Instant Pot Duo Crisp Air Fryer cover?

With the Instant Pot Duo Crisp Air Fryer, you can have your traditional pressure cooker, steamer, slow cooker, food warmer, and sauté pan all in one kitchen device. Added to these, you can also make use of it as an air fryer, broiler, mini-oven, food dehydrator, and broiler.

4. Are there foods I should avoid putting into the Instant Pot?

Foods that are high in sugar content may trigger the Instant Pot to give out a burn alert. Also, extra caution is highly recommended when cooking food like applesauce, oatmeal, pearl barley, and noodles that tend to froth, splatter, or foam as they can cause clogging. When preparing these types of foods, make sure not to fill it beyond the 1/2 line as indicated in the inner pot.

To ensure longevity, regular cleaning of the lids and all their parts are important for proper functioning.

5. Can I use accessories from other brands with my Instant Pot Duo Crisp Air Fryer?

It is recommended that you purchase accessories and other spare parts only from stores authorized by Instant Pot Brands Inc. to ensure the highest level of safety.

Chapter 2 Breakfast and Lunch

Air-fried Scotch Eggs

Preparation Time: 5 minutes
Cooking Time: 15 minutes
Yields: 6 servings
Ingredients
- 1 egg, lightly beaten
- 1 lb. bulk sausage, uncooked
- 5 hard-boiled eggs
- 1 tbsp. mustard or hot sauce
- Oil spray, for coating
- 1 cup almond flour or coconut flour

Directions
1. Peel the hard-boiled eggs and set aside.
2. Meanwhile, divide the sausage into 6 equal parts and flatten to form a 4-inch wide patty. Lay the boiled eggs in the center and wrap the patty around it. Repeat the process until you have used up all the eggs and sausage patties.
3. Dip each sausage-wrapped patty in the beaten egg and then into almond flour for coating. Spray evenly all sides with oil.
4. Place wrapped patties in the air fryer, making sure they aren't overcrowded. You may use the second layer of the air fryer basket to accommodate all patties. Attach the instant pot duo crisp Air Fryer Lid and air fry at 400 degrees F for 12-16 minutes, turning halfway through cooking.
5. Once done, cut in halves and serve with mustard on top. You may also serve it with hot sauce.

Nutritional Information (as per serving): Calories - 407 kcal; Fat - 29.44 g; Carbohydrates - 10.65 g; Protein - 24.91 g; Sugar - 1.59 g; Fiber - 3.3 g; Sodium - 793 mg

Simple & Easy Mac and Cheese

Preparation: 20 minutes
Cooking: 25 minutes
Yields: 6 servings

Ingredients

- 2½ cups macaroni
- 2⅔ cups sharp cheddar or pepper jack, shredded
- 1 cup bread crumbs
- 2 cups chicken stock
- 1¼ cups heavy cream
- ⅓ cup Parmesan cheese, shredded
- 8 tbsps. butter, melted and divided
- ¼ tsp. garlic powder
- Salt and pepper to taste

Directions

1. Place the metal inner pot in your instant pot and add the chicken broth.
2. Also add the heavy cream, 4 tablespoons of butter and macaroni.
3. Pressure cook on HIGH for about 20 minutes or until al dente.
4. Combine the bread crumbs with the remaining butter in a mixing bowl.
5. Quick-release the pressure and stir in 2 cups of sharp cheddar (or pepper jack), salt, pepper and garlic powder.
6. Top with the remaining ⅔ cup of sharp cheddar (or pepper jack), ⅓ cup of Parmesan cheese, and breadcrumb mixture.
7. Air fry at 400 degrees F for about 5 minutes or until browned.
8. Transfer into serving plates and enjoy!

Nutritional Information (as per serving): Calories – 680; Carbohydrates – 22g; Fat – 56g; Fiber – 1g; Protein – 22g; Sodium –765mg; Sugar – 3g

Instant Pot Pepperoni Pasta

Preparation: 5 minutes
Cooking: 25 minutes
Yields: 8 servings

Ingredients

- 16 oz. rigatoni pasta
- 1 lb. Italian sausage
- 6 oz. pepperoni, sliced
- 1 (28 oz.) can diced Italian tomatoes, with juice
- 1 (28 oz.) can tomato puree
- 8 oz. Mozzarella cheese, shredded
- 2 cups chicken stock
- 1 cup red wine
- 1 medium onion, chopped
- 2 tbsps. garlic, minced
- ½ tsp. oregano
- ½ tsp. basil
- ¼ tsp. red pepper, crushed
- ¼ tsp. ground black pepper
- ½ tsp. salt

Directions

1. Set the instant pot to SAUTE then cook the onions, sausage and garlic until browned.
2. Stir in the spices, salt, pepper, the chicken stock, red wine, and half of the pepperoni. Make sure that everything is well combined.
3. Add the tomato puree and tomatoes and stir lightly.
4. Pour in the pasta, gently pressing down to ensure that it's covered with liquid. Don't stir so that the pasta will be kept at the bottom of the pot.
5. Pressure cook on HIGH for about 6 minutes or until al dente.
6. Quick-release and remove the lid.
7. Add in ⅓ of the cheese then stir well. Add the remaining cheese on top and layer the rest of the pepperoni on top of the cheese.
8. Attach the air fryer lid to the instant pot and air-fry at 400 degrees F for 5 minutes.
9. Once cooked, remove the lid and serve the pepperoni pasta.

Nutritional Information (as per serving): Calories – 581; Carbohydrates – 42g; Fat – 33g; Fiber – 4g; Protein – 29g; Sodium – 1218mg; Sugar – 14g

Big Bite Sandwich

Preparation: 5 minutes
Cooking: 13 minutes
Yields: 6 sandwiches

Ingredients
- 6 Italian sausages
- 1½ cups of water
- 6 hot dog buns

Directions
1. Pour about 1½ cups of water into the inner steel pot. Set the trivet and the basket inside the pot, coating the bottom part of the basket with nonstick spray.
2. Place the sausage links inside, making sure that they're not overlapping each other.
3. Close the pot with pressure cooker lid and steam valve. Adjust the setting to HIGH and cook for 5 minutes.
4. Quick-release and remove the lid then spritz the links with cooking spray.
5. Cover the lid and air fry at 400 degrees F for 8 minutes. Flip halfway through the cooking process so that both sides get browned.
6. Remove from the pot and serve in buns.

Nutritional Information (as per sandwich): Calories – 408; Carbohydrates – 26.5g; Fat – 24.7g; Fiber – 0.1g; Protein – 20g; Sodium – 1232mg; Sugar – 2.7g

Cheesy Air Fryer Spaghetti

Preparation: 10 minutes
Cooking: 14 minutes
Yields: 6 servings

Ingredients

- 1 lb. ground beef
- 1 (24 oz.) jar spaghetti sauce
- 8 oz. spaghetti noodles, broken into thirds
- 1½ cups Mozzarella cheese, grated and divided
- ½ cup Parmesan cheese grated
- 2 cups beef broth
- 1 onion, diced
- 1 green onion, diced (optional)
- 2 tbsps. olive oil
- ¼ tsp. salt

Directions

1. Set the instant pot to SAUTE then drizzle the bottom of the steel pot with olive oil.
2. Sauté the onions and ground beef then season with salt. Continue to cook until the ground beef is no longer pink.
3. Evenly spread the cooked meat to cover the bottom of the pot entirely.
4. Pour the spaghetti sauce then add the broth into the jar. Put the lid back on and shake the jar to mix the meat and broth with the remaining sauce. Pour the broth into the pot but do not stir.
5. Sprinkle the broken spaghetti noodles on top of the liquid.
6. Using a spoon spatula, gently submerge the noodles into the sauce but do not stir.
7. Place the pressure cooker lid and close the steam valve.
8. Pressure cook on HIGH for 9 minutes.
9. Quick-release and remove the lid.
10. Stir in one cup of mozzarella cheese until it melts.
11. Sprinkle the remaining half cup of the mozzarella cheese plus the parmesan on top of the spaghetti. Top with the diced green onions then closes the pot with air fryer lid.
12. Air fry at 400degrees F for 5 minutes, until the cheese melts and gets golden brown on top.
13. Serve and enjoy.

Nutritional Information (as per serving): Calories – 338; Carbohydrates – 37g; Fat – 14g; Fiber – 3g; Protein – 16g; Sodium – 1104mg; Sugar – 7g

Healthy Breakfast Bake

Preparation: 6 minutes
Cooking: 25 minutes
Yields: 2 servings

Ingredients

- 1 slice whole grain bread, torn into pieces
- 4 eggs
- 1½ cups baby spinach
- ¼ cup + 2 tbsps. shredded cheddar cheese, divided
- ½ cup bell pepper, diced
- 2 tbsps. 1% low-fat milk
- 1 tsp. hot sauce
- ½ tsp. Kosher salt

Directions

1. Preheat your air fryer to 250 degrees F. Spritz a 6-inch soufflé dish with nonstick spray and set aside.
2. In a medium bowl, add the beaten eggs, hot sauce, milk and salt.
3. Gently fold in the spinach, ¼ cup cheddar, bread pieces and bell peppers.
4. Pour the egg mixture into the prepared soufflé dish and place the dish into the air fryer basket.
5. Set up the trivet to the inner pot of the cooker and place the basket on top.
6. Cook at 250 degrees F for 20 minutes. Sprinkle the top with the remaining cheese and cook for another 5 minutes or until the eggs are set and the edges are golden brown.
7. Remove from the air fryer basket and set aside for about 10 minutes before serving.

Nutritional Information (as per serving): Calories – 173; Carbohydrates – 14g; Fat – 9g; Fiber – 3g; Protein – 9g; Sodium – 524mg; Sugar – 2g

Perfect Bacon & Croissant Breakfast

Preparation: 5 minutes
Cooking: 10 minutes
Yields: 2 bacon-croissant sandwiches

Ingredients

- 4 pieces thick-cut bacon
- 2 croissants, sliced
- 2 eggs
- 1 tbsp. butter

For the bacon barbecue sauce:

- ½ cup ketchup
- 2 tbsps. apple cider vinegar
- 1 tbsp. brown sugar
- 1 tbsp. molasses
- ½ tbsp. Worcestershire sauce
- ¼ tsp. onion powder
- ¼ tsp. mustard powder
- ¼ tsp. liquid smoke

Directions

1. Preheat your air fryer to 390 degrees F.
2. Meanwhile, incorporate all the barbecue sauce ingredients in a small saucepan. Place the pan over medium heat and bring it to a simmer until the sauce thickens slightly.
3. Place the bacon cuts flat on a tray and brush them with barbecue sauce on one side.
4. Transfer to the air fryer basket with the brushed-side up. Cook for about 4-5 minutes then flip the bacon. Brush the other side with bacon sauce and cook for another 5 minutes (or until your desired doneness is achieved).
5. In a medium-size frying pan, melt the butter and fry the eggs according to your preference.
6. Once done, place the eggs at the bottom of each croissant. Top them with two bacon slices each and close with the croissant on top.
7. Serve with your favorite breakfast beverage.

Nutritional Information (per bacon-croissant sandwich): Calories – 643; Carbohydrates – 57g; Fat – 39g; Fiber – 1g; Protein – 16g; Sodium – 1262mg; Sugar – 33g

Air-fried French Toast Sticks

Preparation: 5 minutes
Cooking: 12 minutes
Yields: 2 servings

Ingredients

- 4 pcs. sandwich bread
- 2 tbsps. butter, softened
- 2 eggs, gently beaten
- 1 pinch ground cloves
- 1 pinch cinnamon
- 1 pinch nutmeg
- 1 pinch salt
- 1 tsp. maple syrup, for garnish

Directions

1. Preheat your air fryer to 350 degrees F.
2. Meanwhile, add the beaten eggs, cinnamon, nutmeg, ground cloves and salt in a bowl.
3. Butter both sides of the bread slices and cut them into strips.
4. Dredge each bread strip in the egg mixture, letting the excess liquid mixture drip completely. Arrange them in your air fryer basket; work in two batches if necessary.
5. Place the air fryer trivet in the inner steel pot of your cooker and place the basket on top of it.
6. Air fry for 2 minutes and generously spritz the sticks with cooking spray. Flip the sticks and spray the other side as well.
7. Air fry for another 4 minutes, keeping an eye on them just to make sure they don't burn. They're done when the sticks are golden brown.
8. Remove from the air fryer and transfer to a serving plate. Drizzle with maple syrup before serving. If desired, you can also sprinkle them with icing sugar and top with whip cream.

Nutritional Information (as per serving): Calories – 163; Carbohydrates – 2g; Fat – 15g; Fiber – 0.4g; Protein – 5g; Sodium – 193mg; Sugar – 1g

Ranchero Brunch Crunch Wraps

Preparation: 5 minutes
Cooking: 15 minutes
Yields: 2 crunch wraps

Ingredients

- 2 servings tofu scramble (or vegan egg)
- 2 large flour tortillas
- 2 small corn tortillas
- ⅓ cup pinto beans, cooked
- ½ cup classic ranchero sauce
- ½ avocado, peeled and sliced
- 2 fresh jalapeños, stemmed and sliced

Directions

1. Assemble the large tortillas on a work surface. Arrange the crunch wraps by stacking the following ingredients in order: tofu or egg scramble, jalapeños, ranchero sauce, corn tortillas, avocado, and pinto beans. You can add more ranchero sauce if desired.
2. Fold the large flour tortilla around the fillings until sealed completely.
3. Place one crunch wrap in the air fryer basket and set the basket on top of the trivet.
4. Air-fry each crunch wrap at 350 degrees F (or 180°C) for 6 minutes. Remove from the basket and transfer to a plate.
5. Repeat step 3 and 4 for the other crunch wrap.

Nutritional Information (per crunch wrap): Calories – 290; Carbohydrates – 26g; Fat – 14g; Fiber – 11g; Protein – 15g; Sodium – 340mg; Sugar – 3g

Crunchy Breakfast Nuggets

Preparation: 20 minutes
Cooking: 30 minutes
Yields: 4 servings

Ingredients

- 1 lb. boneless, skinless chicken breasts
- ⅔ cup whole wheat panko bread crumbs
- ⅓ cup Parmesan cheese, freshly grated
- ¼ cup whole wheat flour
- 1 large egg
- 2 tsps. dried parsley flakes
- Olive oil spray
- ¼ tsp. salt or to taste
- ¼ tsp. black pepper

For dipping sauce (optional):

- 1 tbsp. marinara
- 1 tbsp. ranch dressing
- 1 tbsp. barbecue sauce

Directions

1. Preheat your air fryer 400 degrees F for about 8-10 minutes. Meanwhile, slice the chicken breasts into 1-inch cubes.
2. Prepare three shallow bowls; mix the flour, salt, and pepper in the first bowl. Lightly beat the egg in the second and combine the parmesan, panko, and parsley flakes in the third.
3. Working one piece at a time, dredge the chicken in the flour mixture and press lightly to adhere. Next, dip it into the egg, removing the excess egg as needed. Finally, coat with the Panko mixture, pressing lightly to help evenly coat the chicken.
4. Arrange the nuggets in the air fryer basket in a single layer. Liberally spritz them with cooking spray to help them get crispy and golden brown.
5. Air-fry each batch for about 7 minutes or until the internal temperature reaches 165 degrees F (or 74°C). Monitor them to make sure that they're not overcooked.
6. Serve with your favorite dip and your favorite side dish.

Nutritional Information (per 5 nuggets): Calories – 402; Carbohydrates – 34g; Fat – 8g; Fiber – 5g; Protein – 46g; Sodium – 434mg; Sugar – 1g

Air Fryer Garlic Bread

Preparation: 5 minutes
Cooking: 5 minutes
Yields: 4 slices

Ingredients

- 4 slices Ciabatta
- ¼ cup Parmesan, freshly grated
- 1 tbsp. salted butter
- 3 cloves garlic, crushed
- A few pinches of dried parsley

Directions

1. Preheat your air fryer to 360 degrees F.
2. Put the butter in a small bowl and microwave for 10 seconds or until softened.
3. Add the cheese, garlic and dried parsley to the bowl of butter.
4. Spread the garlic mixture to both sides of Ciabatta slices.
5. Assemble the slices in the air fryer basket and air-fry for about 3-5 minutes.
6. Serve warm.

Nutritional Information (per 2 slices): Calories – 288; Carbohydrates – 35g; Fat – 12g; Fiber – 3g; Protein – 10g; Sodium – 629mg; Sugar – 4g

Chapter 3 Vegan and Vegetarian

Crispy Air-Fried Brussels Sprouts

Preparation Time: 5 minutes
Cooking Time: 16 minutes
Yields: 2 servings
Ingredients
- 2 tbsps. Parmesan, freshly grated
- ½ lb. Brussels sprouts, thinly sliced
- 1 tsp. garlic powder
- 1 tbsp. extra-virgin olive oil
- Caesar dressing for dipping
- Freshly ground black pepper to taste
- Kosher salt to taste

Directions
1. Add oil, Brussels sprouts, garlic powder and Parmesan in a large mixing bowl. Toss to combine thoroughly. Season with salt and pepper.
2. Put the coated sprouts in the air fryer basket.
3. Insert trivet into your instant pot and lay the air fryer basket on top. Attach the air fryer lid and cook at 350 degrees F for 8 minutes. Toss and cook for another 8 minutes until sprouts are crisp and golden brown.
4. Garnish with Parmesan. You can serve with Caesar salad for a dip.

Nutritional Information (as per serving): Calories – 202 kcal; Carbohydrates – 15.9 g; Fat – 12.32 g; Protein – 6.89 g; Sugar – 4.18 g; Sodium – 330 mg

Air-fried Green Beans

Preparation Time: 5 minutes
Cook Time: 15 minutes
Yields: 4 servings

Ingredients

- 1 tbsp. olive oil or cooking spray
- 1 lb. fresh green beans (with ends trimmed and cut into halves)
- ½ tsp. garlic powder
- Salt and pepper to taste
- 2 fresh lemon slices

Directions

1. Combine the green beans with garlic powder in a bowl and season with salt and pepper.
2. Arrange the seasoned green beans in the air fryer basket.
3. Place the basket inside the instant pot duo crisp and attach the air fryer lid. Make sure it locks before setting it to air frying mode. Cook at 360 degrees F for 10-14 minutes. Toss and shake two times while cooking. Adjust the seasonings to taste if needed.
4. Garnish with lemon slices and serve.

Nutritional Information (as per serving): Calories - 82 kcal; Fat - 5.66 g; Carbohydrates - 6.3 g; Protein - 1.5 g; Sugar - 1.7 g; Fiber - 2.4 g; Sodium - 46 mg

Roasted Asparagus

Prep Time: 4 minutes
Cook Time: 10 minutes
Yields: 4 servings

Ingredients

- 1 lb. asparagus with ends trimmed and cut into pieces
- 1-2 tsps. olive oil
- Salt and black pepper to taste

Directions

1. Place the asparagus pieces in a shallow dish and coat them with olive oil. Season with salt and pepper. Make sure to properly coat the asparagus ends to prevent them from burning or drying out quickly.
2. Place asparagus inside the air fryer basket and put inside the instant pot duo crisp. Choose the air fryer lift for cover, secure, and set to air frying at 380 degrees F for 7-10 minutes. Shake basket halfway through cooking to cook asparagus evenly.
3. Taste for seasoning and tenderness. Adjust if needed.
4. Serve warm.

Nutritional Information (as per serving): Calories – 52 kcal; Fat – 1.97 g; Carbohydrates – 5.72 g; Protein – 2.95 g; sugar – 2.4 g; Fiber – 2.4 g; Sodium – 273 mg

Air Fryer Crispy Broccoli

Preparation Time: 5 minutes
Cooking Time: 15 minutes
Yields: 4 servings

Ingredients

- 2 tbsps. cooking oil
- 1 lb. broccoli, cut into bite-sized pieces
- ½ tsp. garlic powder
- Salt and pepper to taste
- 2 fresh lemon wedges

Directions

1. Add broccoli to a large bowl and drizzle evenly with olive oil.
2. Season broccoli with garlic powder, salt and pepper.
3. Put in the instant pot duo crisp air fryer basket and cover with the air fryer lid.
4. Air Fry at 380 degrees F for 12-15 minutes, flipping and shaking 3 times through cooking and cook until crispy.
5. Serve with lemon wedges.

Nutritional Information (as per serving): Calories – 104 kcal; Fat – 7.41g; Carbohydrates – 5.42 g; Protein –3.93 g; sugar –1.32 g; Fiber – 3.3 g; Sodium – 39 mg

Air Fried Acorn Squash

Preparation Time: 15 minutes
Cooking Time: 20 minutes
Yields: 4 servings

Ingredients
- 1 acorn squash
- 3 tbsps. butter, melted
- 2 tsps. brown sugar
- ½ tsp. Kosher salt
- Black pepper to taste
- Optional toppings: melted butter, roasted nuts (chopped), pomegranate seeds

Direction
1. Cleanse the squash and trim the ends. Cut in half and core to remove seeds. Cut into about half an inch thick.
2. Combine brown sugar and melted butter in a bowl. Season with salt and pepper.
3. Add in the acorn squash and toss to coat.
4. Place the coated squash into the air fryer basket and attach the air fryer lid to the instant pot. Set to air fry at 375 degrees F for 15-20 minutes or until tender, flipping after 10 minutes of cooking.
5. Once done, serve in a platter drizzled with melted butter, pomegranate seeds and chopped nuts. Taste for seasoning and adjust flavor if needed.

Nutritional Information (as per serving): Calories – 191 kcal; Fat – 7.73; Carbohydrates – 27.74 g; Protein –2.63 g; sugar –12.45 g; Fiber – 4.6 g; Sodium – 352 mg

Air-fried Avocado

Preparation Time: 10 minutes
Cooking Time: 10 minutes
Yields: 2 servings

Ingredients

- ½ cup all-purpose flour
- 2 avocados
- 2 large eggs
- 2 tbsps. canola mayonnaise
- 1 tbsp. apple cider vinegar
- 1 tbsp. Sriracha chili sauce
- 1½ tsps. black pepper
- ¼ tsp. Kosher salt
- ½ cup Panko bread crumbs
- ¼ cup no-salt-added ketchup
- 1 tbsp. water
- Cooking spray

Directions

1. Cut avocados into 4 wedges each. Prepare 3 shallow dishes.
2. In the first shallow dish, combine avocado wedges with flour and pepper.
3. In another dish, lightly beat eggs.
4. Place bread crumbs in the third dish.
5. First, dredge avocado wedges in the flour mixture, one after the other. After coating with flour, shake lightly to remove excess flour and dip the avocado to the egg mixture, likewise shaking lightly to drip off excess liquid. Finally, dip each wedge to the bread crumbs coating them evenly on all sides and spray with cooking oil.
6. Arrange avocado wedges in the instant pot duo air fryer basket, place inside the pot, and cover with the air fryer lid. Set to air fry at 400 degrees F until wedges turn golden brown, turning them over halfway through cooking. Remove avocado wedges from the fryer and sprinkle them with salt.
7. Meanwhile, while waiting for the avocado wedges to get cooked, mix mayonnaise, ketchup, apple cider vinegar, water and Sriracha sauce in a small bowl.
8. Serve the prepared sauce with the avocado wedges while still warm.

Nutritional Information (as per serving): Calories – 274 kcal; Fat – 18g; Carbohydrates – 23g; Protein –5g; sugar –5g; Fiber – 7g; Sodium – 306mg

Mediterranean Veggies

Preparation Time: 5 minutes
Cooking Time: 20 minutes
Yields: 4 servings

Ingredients

- 1 large courgette
- 2 oz. cherry tomatoes
- 1 green pepper
- 1 medium carrot
- 1 large parsnip
- 1 tsp. mixed herbs
- 2 tbsps. honey
- 3 tbsps. olive oil
- 2 tsps. garlic puree
- 1 tsp. mustard
- Salt and pepper to taste

Directions

1. Slice up the courgette and the green pepper.
2. Peel and dice the carrot and the parsnip.
3. Add them all altogether in the air fryer basket of the instant pot duo along with raw cherry tomatoes, herbs, garlic puree, mustard, salt and pepper. Drizzle with three tablespoons of olive oil.
4. Place the air fryer in the pot and air fry for 15 minutes at 356 degrees F using the instant pot duo crisp air fryer. Sprinkle with more salt if needed and serve.

Nutritional Information (as per serving): Calories – 281 kcal; Fat – 21g; Carbohydrates – 21g; Protein –2g; sugar –13g; Fiber – 3g; Sodium – 36mg

Rosemary Air-fried Potatoes

Preparation Time: 10 minutes
Cooking Time: 15 minutes
Yields: 4 servings

Ingredients

- 3 tbsps. vegetable oil
- 4 yellow baby potatoes, quartered
- 2 tsps. dried rosemary, minced
- 1 tbsp. minced garlic
- 1 tsp. ground black pepper
- ¼ cup chopped parsley
- 1 tbsp. fresh lime or lemon juice
- 1 tsp. salt

Directions

1. Add potatoes, garlic, rosemary, oil, pepper, and salt in a large bowl. Mix thoroughly.
2. Arrange seasoned potatoes in the air fryer basket and place inside the instant pot duo. Cover with the air fryer lid and air-fry at 400 degrees F for about 15 minutes.
3. Check to see if potatoes are cooked through.
4. Once cooked, take it out of the air fryer and place in a platter.
5. Sprinkle with lemon juice and parsley.
6. Serve warm.

Nutritional Information (as per serving): Calories – 201 kcal; Fat – 10.71g; Carbohydrates – 22.71g; Protein –3.34g; sugar –1.32g; Fiber – 3.5g; Sodium – 592.97mg

Air Fryer Falafel Balls

Preparation Time: 30 minutes
Cooking Time: 12 minutes
Yields: 3 servings
Ingredients
- ½ cup sweet onion, diced
- 2 tbsps. olive oil
- ½ tsp. turmeric
- ½ cup carrots, minced
- 1 cup rolled oats
- ½ cup roasted and salted cashews
- 2 cups canned chickpeas, drained and rinsed
- Juice of 1 fresh lemon
- 2 tbsps. soy sauce
- 1 tbsp. flax meal
- ½ tsp. garlic powder
- ½ tsp. ground cumin

Directions
1. Put a little olive oil and sauté onions and carrots in the instant pot duo. Cook for about 7 minutes and transfer onions and carrots to a large bowl. Use the pressure cooker lid and do not forget to detach it after using.
2. Place cashews and oats in a food processor and process until you achieve a coarse meal consistency. Add the mixture to the bowl with the vegetables.
3. Next, place chickpeas with the lemon juice and soy sauce into the food processor, puree until semi-smooth in consistency.
4. Transfer to the bowl and add in the flax meal and spices. Stir to blend. Make sure that everything is well mixed.
5. Using your hands, form falafel balls from the dough and arrange them into single layer in the air fryer basket lined with parchment paper. You may use two-layered air fryer to accommodate all in a single batch. Place the air fryer basket into the instant pot and attach the air fryer lid to cover. Secure lock and air-fry at 370 degrees F for 12 minutes. Shake the basket after 8 minutes for even cooking,
6. Serve dish on top of salad greens with Magical Tahini Dressing.

Nutritional Information (as per serving): Calories – 735kcal; Carbohydrates – 74.07 g; Fat – 38.91 g; Protein – 22.02 g; Sugar –15.71 g; Sodium – 316 mg

Air Fried Cauliflower Rice

Preparation Time: 10 minutes
Cooking Time: 15 minutes
Yields: 2 servings

Ingredients

- 2 cups cauliflower florets
- 3 cloves of garlic
- ½ tsp. smoked paprika
- 1 tbsp. peanut oil

Directions

1. Smash garlic using the blade of a knife.
2. Place all ingredients in a mixing bowl and mix to coat cauliflower florets with the seasoning.
3. Line the air fryer basket with parchment paper and place coated florets in it.
4. Insert the basket inside the instant pot duo crisp and attach the Air Fryer Lid.
5. Air fry for 15 minutes at 400 degrees F, shaking the air fryer basket every 5 minutes. If you want it crispier, cook for an additional 5 minutes.
6. Serve and enjoy!

Nutritional Information (as per serving): Calories – 129.8 kcal; Carbohydrates – 12.4g; Fat – 7 g; Protein – 4.3 g; Sugar – 5 g; Sodium –642 mg

Chapter 4 Fish and Seafood

Crisp-fried Salmon

Preparation Time: 5 minutes
Cooking Time: 10 minutes
Yields: 2 servings
Ingredients
- ½ tsp. thyme leaves
- 1 tsp. brown sugar
- 2 tbsps. whole grain mustard
- Freshly ground black pepper and salt to taste
- 2 (6 oz.) salmon fillets
- 2 tsps. extra-virgin olive oil
- 1 clove of garlic, minced

Directions
1. Rub salmon with salt and pepper.
2. In a small mixing bowl, add the mustard, garlic, sugar, thyme and oil. Whisk to blend. Spread the mixture on top of the salmon.
3. Arrange salmon in the air fryer basket and the set air fryer to 400 degrees F. Cook for 10 minutes until the salmon turns brown and crispy.
4. Serve and enjoy.

Nutritional Information (as per serving): Calories – 317 kcal; Carbohydrates – 10.33 g; Fat – 14.38 g; Protein – 36.66 g; Sugar – 3.42 g; Sodium – 778 mg

Air Fryer Tuna Patties

Preparation Time: 15 minutes
Cook Time: 10 minutes
Yields: 8 servings

Ingredients

- ½ tsp. dried herbs: oregano, dill, basil, thyme or any combo
- 2-3 large eggs
- 15 oz. canned tuna, drained
- Zest of 1 medium lemon
- Freshly cracked black pepper to taste
- ½ cup bread crumbs
- 1 tbsp. lemon juice
- 3 tbsps. grated Parmesan cheese
- 3 tbsps. onion, minced
- 1 stalk of celery, finely chopped
- ½ tsp. garlic powder
- Optional tartar sauce, ranch, lemon slices, mayonnaise for serving
- ¼ tsp. Kosher salt
- 2 lemon slices for garnish

Directions

1. Combine eggs, Parmesan cheese, bread crumbs, lemon zest, lemon juice, garlic powder, onions, celery, and dried herbs in a bowl. Season with salt and pepper to taste. Gently fold in the tuna and stir thoroughly to combine.
2. Form the mixture into 3" x 3" patties. This recipe makes about 10 patties. If the patties turn out too soft, chill in the fridge for about an hour to harden.
3. Line each layer of the air fryer basket with parchment paper and spray with olive oil before arranging patties inside in a single layer to avoid overcrowding.
4. Lay the second layer of the air fryer basket with patties on top of the first layer. Also, spray with olive oil.
5. Place the 2-layered air fryer basket inside the instant pot unit and cover with the air fryer lid.
6. Air-fry for about 10 minutes at 360 degrees F, flipping halfway. Spray with olive oil after flipping.
7. Garnish with lemon slices and serve with your favorite sauce.

Nutritional Information (as per serving): Calories - 68 kcal; Fat - 2.29 g; Carbohydrates - 2.33 g; Protein - 9.63 g; Sugar - 0.5 g; Fiber - 0.5 g; Sodium - 213 mg

Air Fryer Garlic-lemon Shrimp

Preparation Time: 10 minutes
Cooking Time: 15 minutes
Yields: 2-3 servings

Ingredients
- 1 lb. raw shrimp, peeled and deveined
- ¼ tsp. garlic powder
- 2 lemon wedges, juiced
- 1 tablespoon vegetable oil or spray for coating
- Salt and black pepper to taste
- A pinch of parsley, minced
- Optional: a dash of chili flakes

Directions
1. Add shrimp in a bowl. Pour oil and toss to combine.
2. Add garlic powder and season with salt and pepper. Toss to coat evenly.
3. Place shrimp in a single-layered instant pot air fryer basket.
4. Attach to the instant pot duo crisp air fryer lid and securely cover the pot.
5. Set to air frying mode and cook at 400 degrees F for 10-14 minutes, flipping halfway for even cooking.
6. Once the timer is off or when the shrimp is cooked, transfer to a plate and squeeze lemon juice over it.
7. Sprinkle with parsley or chili flakes or both.
8. Serve while hot.

Nutritional Information (as per serving): Calories - 243 kcal; Fat - 4.34 g; Carbohydrates - 4.11 g; Protein - 46.93 g; Sugar - 1.77 g; Fiber - 0.5 g; Sodium - 1975 mg

Air Fried White Fish with Garlic & Lemon

Preparation Time: 5 minutes
Cooking Time: 10 minutes
Servings: 2 servings

Ingredients

- Freshly cracked black pepper to taste
- ½ tsp. lemon powder
- 12 oz. tilapia fillets or white fish
- 1 tablespoon freshly chopped parsley
- ½ tsp. garlic powder
- 4 lemon wedges
- ½ tsp. onion powder, optional
- Salt to taste

Direction

1. Cleanse and pat dry fish fillets. Coat with olive oil and season with onion powder, garlic powder and lemon powder. Season with salt and pepper. Make sure fillets are evenly coated.
2. Line air fryer basket with parchment paper and lightly grease with cooking spray.
3. Arrange fish on top, adding few lemon wedges. Insert the air fryer basket to the instant pot duo crisp and attach the air fryer lid. Secure lock and air-fry at 360 degrees F for about 6-12 minutes or until fish can be flaked. Expect thicker fillets to take longer time to cook so adjust cooking time.
4. Sprinkle chopped parsley on the cooked dish and serve immediately with roasted lemon wedges.

Nutritional Information (as per serving): Calories - 308 kcal; Fat – 16.47 g; Carbohydrates – 6.88 g; Protein – 33.08 g; Sugar – 2.15 g; Sodium - 208 mg

Air-fried Shrimps with Lemon

Preparation Time: 10 minutes
Cooking Time: 15 minutes
Yields: 2-4 servings

Ingredients

- ¼ tsp. garlic powder
- 1 pound raw shrimps, peeled and deveined
- A dash of vegetable oil or cooking spray, for coating
- A pinch of parsley or chili flakes, optional
- Black pepper and salt to taste
- 2 lemon wedges, juiced

Directions

1. In a bowl, combine shrimps with oil and add salt, pepper and garlic. Toss thoroughly to mix well.
2. Place shrimps in the air fryer basket and insert the basket inside the instant pot. Attach the air fryer lid and set to air-fry at 400 degrees F for 10-14 minutes. Gently shake the air fryer basket to flip halfway through cooking.
3. Once done, transfer the shrimp dish to a bowl and drizzle lemon juice over it.
4. Sprinkle parsley or chili flakes on top and serve hot.

Nutritional Information (as per serving): Calories - 117 kcal; Fat – 1.66 g; Carbohydrates – 2.07 g; Protein – 23.46 g; Sugar – 0.88 g; Sodium – 988 mg

Air-fried Crumbed Fish

Preparation Time: 10 minutes
Cooking Time: 12 minutes
Yields 4: 4 servings

Ingredients:
- ¼ cup vegetable oil
- 1 egg, beaten
- 4 flounder fillets
- 1 cup dry bread crumbs
- 1 lemon, sliced

Directions
1. In a mixing bowl, mix oil and bread crumbs. Stir to combine.
2. Dredge fillets into the egg, shaking off excess liquid.
3. Dip fillets into the bread crumbs to coat evenly on all sides.
4. Lay coated fillets on the air fryer basket and place inside the instant pot. Attach the air fryer lid and cook at 350 degrees F for about 12 minutes. Flip halfway through cooking.
5. Garnish with lemon slices and serve.

Nutritional Information (as per serving): Calories – 357 kcal; Carbohydrates – 22.5g; Fat – 17.7g; Protein – 26.9g; Sugar – 2g; Sodium – 309mg

Air Fryer Coconut Shrimp

Preparation Time: 30 minutes
Cooking Time: 10 minutes
Yields: 6 servings

Ingredients

- 2 large eggs
- ½ tsp. ground black pepper
- 3 cups panko bread crumbs
- ½ cup all-purpose flour
- ¼ cup honey
- 3 cups flaked coconut, unsweetened
- 12 oz. medium-sized raw shrimps, peeled and deveined
- 1 Serrano chili, thinly sliced
- ½ tsp. Kosher salt, divided
- 2 tsps. fresh cilantro, chopped
- ¼ cup lime juice

Directions

1. Combine pepper and flour in a shallow dish. Stir to combine.
2. In another shallow dish, add the lightly beaten eggs.
3. Add coconut and bread crumbs in another shallow dish.
4. Dredge shrimps in the shallow dish with flour. Shake lightly to remove excess flour.
5. One by one, dip shrimp to the dish with the egg mixture. Allow excess liquid to drip off. Transfer to the third dish with coconut-bread crumbs mixture. Coat shrimps evenly on all sides and lay them inside the 2-layered air fryer basket of the instant pot duo crisp lined with parchment paper. Coat shrimps with cooking spray, avoiding overcrowding.
6. Place the air fryer inside the instant pot and cover with air fryer lid. Lock in place and air fry at 200 degrees F for about 3 minutes, flip and cook for another 3 minutes. Season with salt to taste.
7. In a small bowl, combine honey, Serrano chili and lime juice. Whisk together for the dip.
8. Serve crisp shrimps sprinkled with cilantro and the sauce for dipping.

Nutritional Information (as per serving): Calories - 247 kcal; Fat – 9.1 g; Carbohydrates – 27.6 g; Protein – 13.8 g; Sugar – 13 g; Sodium – 316 mg

Air Fryer Fish Sticks

Preparation Time: 10 minutes
Cooking Time: 10 minutes
Yields: 4 servings

Ingredients

- ½ cup all-purpose flour
- 1 lb. white fish fillet, tilapia or cod
- 1 large egg
- ½ cup Parmesan cheese, grated
- ½ cup panko bread crumbs
- 1 tsp. paprika
- 1 tbsp. parsley flakes
- 1 tsp. black pepper
- Cooking spray

Directions

1. Cleanse fish and pat dry with paper towels. Cut into 1"x3" sticks.
2. Prepare 3 shallow dishes. Put flour in the first dish. Beat egg in the second dish and mix Parmesan cheese, panko bread crumbs and seasonings in the third dish.
3. Coat fish sticks evenly with flour and then dip to the dish with beaten eggs. Shake off excess liquid. Dip in the seasoned bread crumbs to coat and shake off excess bread crumbs.
4. Line air fryer basket with parchment paper and spray cooking oil.
5. Arrange fish sticks on the air fryer basket and spray cooking oil on top before putting inside the instant pot. Cover with the air fryer lid and air fry at 400 degrees F for 5 minutes. Flip fish sticks after the timer ended and cook for an additional 5 minutes.
6. Serve in a platter.

Nutritional Information (as per serving): Calories – 208 kcal; Carbohydrates – 16.5.g; Fat – 4.1g; Protein – 26.3g; Sugar – 2g; Sodium – 245 mg

Air Fryer Lobster Tails with Lemon-garlic Butter

Preparation Time: 10 minutes
Cooking Time: 10 minutes
Yields: 2 servings

Ingredients

- 4 tbsps. butter
- 2 (4 oz.) lobster tails
- 1 tsp. lemon zest
- 1 tsp. fresh parsley, chopped
- 1 clove of garlic, minced and grated
- 2 lemon wedges
- Salt and ground black pepper to taste

Directions

1. Use kitchen shears to cut the lobster tails lengthwise through the center hard shell and flesh but not through the other side of the shell.
2. Spread tails apart and place them in the air fryer basket with the lobster's meat facing upward.
3. Add butter, lemon zest and garlic to the instant pot duo and attach the pressure cooker lid. Set to sauté function for 30 seconds. Once the butter has melted and garlic is tender, transfer 2 tablespoons of butter mixture to the small bowl and brush onto the lobster. Season lobster with salt and pepper.
4. Place the air fryer into the instant pot. Detach the pressure cooker lid and attach the air fryer lid and air fry at 380 degrees F for 5-7 minutes.
5. Once done, remove the lobster tails from the air fryer and transfer to a platter. Spoon some melted butter from the inner pot over the dish and top with lemon wedges and parsley.

Nutritional Information (as per serving): Calories – 318 kcal; Fat – 25.8g; Carbohydrates – 3.3g; Protein – 18.1 g; sugar – 18.97g; Fiber – 3.6g; Sodium – 590 mg

Air Fried Shrimps

Preparation Time: 5 minutes
Cooking Time: 8 minutes
Yields: 4 servings

Ingredients
- 1 lb. large shrimps, peeled and deveined
- 1 tbsp. butter
- ½ tsp. garlic granules
- 1 tsp. lemon juice
- 1/8 cup Parmesan cheese, freshly grated
- 1/8 tsp. salt

Directions
1. Remove shrimps' tails.
2. Mix in garlic granules, lemon, and salt to a bowl with the melted butter.
3. Add the shrimps and toss to coat evenly on all sides.
4. Line the air fryer basket with parchment paper and place shrimps inside. Sprinkle Parmesan cheese over shrimps.
5. Place the air fryer basket inside the instant pot duo crisp and attach the air fryer lid.
6. Set to air fry at 400 degrees F for 8 minutes. Cook until shrimps become bright red and the meat is opaque.

Nutritional Information (per 2 slices): Calories –122 kcal; Carbohydrates – 0.5g; Fat – 4.6g; Protein – 19.6g; Sodium – 330mg;

Crisp Shrimp ala Bang Bang

Preparation Time: 15 minutes
Cooking Time: 12 minutes
Yields: 4 servings

Ingredients
- 1 lb. raw shrimps, peeled and deveined
- ½ cup mayonnaise
- 1 tbsp. Sriracha sauce
- ¼ cup sweet chili sauce
- 1 head loose lettuce
- ¼ cup all-purpose flour
- Optional: 2 green onions, chopped
- 1 cup panko bread crumbs

Directions
1. For the bang bang sauce, add chili sauce, mayonnaise, and Sriracha sauce in a mixing bowl and whisk until smooth. Reserve some of the sauce for dipping if desired.
2. Place flour on a shallow dish and panko bread crumbs on another shallow dish.
3. Coat shrimps evenly on all sides with flour and then dip to the dish of bread crumbs.
4. Place coated shrimps in the air fryer basket lined with parchment paper. Repeat the process for all the remaining shrimps and avoid overcrowding in the air fryer. If there's not enough space for one-layer, use the second layer of the air fryer basket to accommodate all the shrimps.
5. Place the air fryer basket with the coated shrimps inside the pot and attach the air fryer lid.
6. Air-fry at 500 degrees F for 12 minutes.
7. Serve in a platter wraps in lettuce and garnished with green onions.

Nutritional Information (per 2 slices): Calories –442 kcal; Carbohydrates – 32.7g; Fat – 23.9g; Protein – 23.9g; Sugar - 3g; Sodium – 894mg

Air-fryer Cajun Salmon

Preparation Time: 10 minutes
Cooking Time: 10 minutes
Yields: 2 servings
Ingredients:
- 2 (6 oz.) salmon fillets, skin included
- 1 tsp. brown sugar
- 1 tbsp. Cajun seasoning
- Cooking spray

Directions
1. Rinse salmon fillets and pat dry with paper towels.
2. In a small mixing bowl, combine Cajun seasoning and brown sugar. Dip fillets into the mixture, coating evenly all sides.
3. Lay coated fillets on the air frying basket with skin-side down and mist with cooking spray.
4. Place air frying basket inside the instant pot duo crisp and attach the air fryer lid. Set to air fry at 390 degrees F and cook for 8 minutes.
5. Remove from the air fryer and set aside for 2 minutes before serving.

Nutritional Information (per 2 slices): Calories –122 kcal; Carbohydrates – 0.5g; Fat – 4.6g; Protein – 19.6g; Sodium – 330mg

Chapter 5 Beef, Lamb, and Pork

Air Fryer Steak

Preparation Time: 25 minutes
Cooking Time: 14 minutes
Yields: 2 servings
Ingredients
- 2 lbs. bone-in-rib eye
- 2 cloves garlic
- 4 tbsps. butter, softened
- 1 tsp. fresh parsley, chopped
- 1 tsp. fresh chives
- 1 tsp. fresh rosemary, chopped
- 1 tsp. fresh thyme, chopped
- Salt and pepper to taste

Directions
1. Combine herbs and butter in a bowl.
2. Lay a plastic wrap on a flat surface and place the mixture into its center. Roll up and twist its ends to tighten. Chill in the fridge for about 20 minutes.
3. Rub steaks with salt and pepper on both sides.
4. Place in the air fryer basket and place over the trivet inside the pot.
5. Attach the air fryer lid and cook at 400 degrees F for 12-14 minutes, flipping halfway through.
6. You may have a slice of herb butter for the topping. Garnish with parsley and chives.
7. Serve and enjoy.

Nutritional Information (as per serving): Calories – 829 kcal; Fat – 87.28 g; Carbohydrates – 1.22 g; Protein – 9.63 g; Sugar – 0.4 g; Fiber – 0.2 g; Sodium – 363 mg

Italian-style Air-fried Meatballs

Preparation Time: 25 minutes
Cooking Time: 15 minutes
Yields: 12 servings

Ingredients

- 1 medium-size shallot, minced
- 2 tbsps. olive oil
- 2 tbsps. whole milk
- 2 onions, chopped
- 3 cloves garlic, minced
- 2/3 lb. lean ground beef
- 1 large egg, lightly beaten
- ⅓ lb. bulk turkey sausage
- ¼ cup fresh flat-leaf parsley, finely chopped
- 1 tbsp. Dijon mustard
- 1 tbsp. fresh thyme, finely chopped
- 1 tbsp. fresh rosemary, finely chopped
- ½ tsp. Kosher salt
- 1 cup panko bread crumbs

Directions

1. Sauté garlic and onions in the Instant Pot using and cover with the Pressure cooker lid. Set to Sauté function and cook for 1-2 minutes. Remove garlic and shallot from the pot.
2. Combine panko bread crumbs and milk in a large bowl and let them stand for about 5 minutes.
3. Mix the shallot and garlic to the breadcrumb mixture together with the turkey sausage, beef, and the rest of the remaining ingredients.
4. Gently shape the batter into 1½-inch balls using your hands. Place meatballs in the air fryer basket lined with parchment paper over a raised trivet inside the Instant Pot. Cook in batches to avoid overcrowding. Cover the instant pot using the air fryer lid this time and set cooking to 400 degrees F for 10-11 minutes. Remove from the basket to cook the remaining meatballs using the same process.

Nutritional Information (as per serving): Calories – 88 kcal; Carbohydrates – 0g; Fat – 8g; Protein – 4g; Sugar – 0g; Sodium – 254mg

Air Fryer Pork Chops

Preparation Time: 5 minutes
Cook Time: 15 minutes
Yields: 3 servings

Ingredients
- 3 (6 oz) pork chops
- 2 tsps. olive oil
- Salt and black pepper to taste
- A dash of paprika

Directions
1. Cleanse pork chops and pat dry. Put in a large mixing bowl and add the olive oil. Add salt and pepper to taste along with paprika and combine to allow the flavor to seep through the pork chops. Leave for a while to marinate.
2. Place the air fryer basket in the instant pot and arrange pork chops inside. You don't need to cook in batches as instant pot duo crisp has a two-layered basket to accommodate your recipe in one sitting. Attach the air fryer lid and set to 380 degrees F and cook for 10-14 minutes, flipping pork chops halfway through cooking.
3. Test for tenderness and cook more if you want it to be crispier.
4. Serve warm.

Nutritional Information (as per serving): Calories –378 kcal; Carbohydrates – 1.53g; Fat – 21.87g; Protein – 43.89g; Fiber - 0.3g; Sugar – 0.79g; Sodium – 95mg

Air Fryer Bacon Recipe

Cooking Time: 10 minutes
Yields: 4 servings
Ingredients

- 8 slices of bacon

Directions

1. Arrange bacon slices in a single layer in the instant pot duo crisp air fryer basket.
2. Attach the air fryer lid and set to air frying.
3. Cook at 400 degrees F for 8-10 minutes, flipping halfway through.
4. Serve while crispy.

Nutritional Information (as per serving): Calories – 106 kcal; Carbohydrates – 0.22 g; Fat – 10.21 g; Protein – 3.26 g; Fiber - 0 g; Sugar – 0.22 g; Sodium – 122 mg

Air Fryer Pork Chop Bites with Mushrooms

Preparation Time: 15 minutes
Cooking Time: 20 minutes
Yields: 4 servings

Ingredients

- 2 tbsps. melted butter or olive oil
- 1 lb. pork chops, cleansed and pat dried
- 8 oz. mushrooms, cleansed, washed and halved
- ½ tsp. garlic powder
- 1 tsp. Worcestershire sauce or soy sauce
- Black pepper and salt to taste

Directions

1. Chop pork into ¾-inch cubes and combine with mushrooms. Brush pork and mushrooms with melted butter and add seasonings.
2. Cut the pork chops into ¾-inch-sized cubes and combine with the mushrooms. Coat the pork and mushrooms with melted butter or oil. Season with garlic powder, Worcestershire sauce, salt, and pepper. Spread the pork and mushrooms in even layer in the air fryer basket.
3. Air fry at 400 degrees F for 10-18 minutes, shaking and flipping the pork belly 2 times through cooking process. Check the pork chops to see how well done it is cooked. If you want it crispier, cook for an additional 2-5 minutes.
4. Season with additional salt and pepper if desired.
5. Serve warm.

Nutritional Information (as per serving): Calories – 473 kcal; Carbohydrates – 44.42 g; Fat – 17.23 g; Protein – 35.09 g; Fiber - 6.8 g; Sugar – 2.09 g; Sodium – 122 mg

Air Fryer Pork Belly Bites

Preparation Time: 15 minutes
Cooking Time: 20 minutes
Servings: 4 servings

Ingredients

- 1 lb. pork belly, rinsed and patted dry
- 1 tbsp. Worcestershire sauce or soy sauce
- ½ tsp. garlic powder
- Black pepper and salt to taste
- Optional: ¼ cup BBQ sauce

Directions

1. Cleanse pork belly and remove the skin if any. Cut into ¾-inch cubes and place them in a bowl. Add seasonings and spread pork belly cubes in the air fryer basket.
2. Put the air fryer inside the instant pot duo crisp. Attach the air fryer lid and air fry at 400 degrees F for 10-18 minutes. Shake and flip the air fryer basket for even coating twice through the cooking process, depending on desired crispiness.
3. If you want it to be crispier, extend the cooking time up to 20 minutes.
4. Drizzle with BBQ sauce if desired.

Nutritional Information (as per serving): Calories – 313 kcal; Carbohydrates – 2.35 g; Fat – 20.81 g; Protein – 29 g; Fiber - 0.3 g; Sugar – 1.35 g; Sodium – 127 mg

Air Fryer Steak Bites & Mushrooms

Preparation Time: 10 minutes
Cooking Time: 20 minutes
Yields: 4 servings

Ingredients
- 8 oz. mushrooms, cleaned, washed and halved
- 1 lb. steaks, cut into 1-inch cubes and patted dry
- 2 tbsps. butter, melted
- ½ tsp. garlic powder
- 1 tsp. Worcestershire sauce
- A dash of minced parsley for garnish
- Optional: melted butter or chili flakes for finishing
- Black pepper and salt to taste

Directions
1. Add steak cubes and mushrooms in a bowl and coat with melted butter. Season the dish with garlic powder, Worcestershire sauce, salt and pepper to taste.
2. Arrange mushrooms and steak cubes in the instant pot air fryer basket. Set to air fry at 400 degrees F for 10-18 minutes, flipping from time to time for even cooking.
3. If you desire your steaks to be crispier, cook for an additional 2-5 minutes.
4. Garnish with parsley and drizzle with melted butter or chili flakes if desired. Adjust seasoning with salt and pepper if needed.
5. Serve warm.

Nutritional Information (as per serving): Calories – 471 kcal; Carbohydrates – 44.38g; Fat – 15.94 g; Protein – 37.52 g; Fiber - 1.5 g; Sugar – 1.17 g; Sodium – 481 mg

Air Fryer Steak Tips

Preparation Time: 10 minutes
Cooking Time: 20 minutes
Yields: 4 servings

Ingredients

- ½ lb. potatoes, peeled and cut into half-inch pieces
- 1 lb. steaks, cut into half-inch cubes and pat dry
- 2 tbsps. melted butter, oil for alternative
- 1 tsp. Worcestershire sauce
- ½ tsp. garlic powder
- Salt and black pepper to taste
- A pinch of minced parsley for garnish
- Optional: melted butter or chili flakes for finishing

Directions

1. Add potatoes to the instant pot duo crisp and boil for about 5 minutes or until tender, using the pressure cooker lid. Drain and set aside.
2. In a mixing bowl, toss together potatoes and steak cubes with melted butter, garlic powder, and Worcestershire sauce. Season with salt and pepper to taste.
3. Spread steak cubes and potatoes in the air fryer basket. Using the air fryer lid, air-fry at 400 degrees F for 10-18 minutes, shaking and flipping potatoes halfway through cooking, depending on preferred crispness. If you want your steak cubes to be crispier, cook for another 2-5 minutes.
4. Garnish with parsley, and drizzle with melted butter if desired. You may also use chili flakes.
5. Serve warm.

Nutritional Information (as per serving): Calories – 344 kcal; Carbohydrates – 11.54 g; Fat – 18.39 g; Protein – 33 g; Fiber - 1.5 g; Sugar – 1.17 g; Sodium – 481 mg

Air-fried Garlic-rosemary Lamb Chops

Preparation Time: 3 minutes
Cooking Time: 12 minutes
Yields: 2 servings
Ingredients
- 2 lamb chops
- 1 clove of garlic
- 2 tsps. olive oil
- 2 tsps. garlic puree
- A sprig of fresh rosemary
- Salt and pepper to taste

Directions
1. Place lamb chops in a bowl and season with salt and pepper and brush or spray with olive oil.
2. Top each lamb chop with garlic puree.
3. Between each chops place fresh rosemary and unpeeled garlic.
4. Leave the bowl with the lamb chops in the refrigerator for about an hour to marinate.
5. Transfer the marinated lamb chops to the instant pot duo crisp air fryer basket and air-fry at 360 degrees F for 6 minutes.
6. Flip lamb chops for even cooking and cook for another 6 minutes without changing the cooking temperature.
7. Leave to rest for a minute or 2.
8. Discard the fresh garlic and rosemary and serve.

Nutritional Information (per 2 slices): Calories – 426; Carbohydrates – 1g; Fat – 10g; Protein – 83g; Sodium – 200mg;

Air Fryer Sweet and Sour Pork

Preparation Time: 15 minutes
Cooking Time: 12 minutes
Yields: 4 servings

Ingredients

- 2 lbs. pork, cut into chunks
- 1 cup potato starch
- 3 tbsps. canola oil
- 2 large eggs
- ¼ tsp. Chinese Five Spice
- Sea salt to taste
- 1 tsp. sesame oil, optional
- For Sweet and Sour
- ½ tsp. garlic powder
- 1 tbsp. ketchup
- ½ cup white sugar
- 1 tbsp. low-sodium soy sauce
- ½ cup seasoned rice vinegar

Directions

For Sweet and Sour Sauce

1. To make the sweet and sour sauce, add all sweet and sour sauce ingredients into the instant pot duo and cover with the pressure cooker lid. Set to Sauté mode and cook for about 5 minutes. Transfer to a bowl and reserve for later use.

For the Pork

1. Combine all seasonings in a mixing bowl (pepper, Chinese Five Spice and potato starch).
2. Add beaten eggs and sesame oil in a separate bowl.
3. Dredge pork pieces in the potato starch, shaking off any excess starch. Dip one by one into the egg mixture, again shaking to drip off before dipping back to the potato starch mix.
4. Grease instant pot air fryer basket with oil and arrange pork pieces inside. Spray oil on top and attach the air fryer lid for cover.
5. Set to air fry and cook at 340 degrees F for 8-12 minutes until cooked, shaking air fryer basket halfway through cooking.
6. Serve with Sweet and Sour Sauce.

Nutritional Information (as per serving): Calories – 520 kcal; Carbohydrates – 21.15 g; Fat – 29.99 g; Protein – 41.28 g; Fiber - 1.6 g; Sugar – 7.41 g; Sodium – 2741 mg

Baby Back Ribs

Preparation Time: 15 minutes
Cooking Time: 35 minutes
Yields: 4 servings

Ingredients

- 1 tbsp. olive oil
- 1 rack baby back ribs
- 1 tbsp. liquid smoke flavoring
- 1 tbsp. brown sugar
- ½ tsp. garlic powder
- ½ tsp. chili powder
- 1 cup BBQ sauce
- ½ tsp. ground black pepper
- ½ tsp. onion powder
- ½ tsp. salt

Directions

1. Cleanse ribs by removing membranes on the back part and run through tap water. Pat dry with a paper towel. Cut ribs into 4 portions.
2. In a mixing bowl, combine liquid smoke with oil and rub ribs on both sides.
3. Add pepper, brown sugar, garlic powder, onion powder, chili powder in a mixing bowl. Also, add salt and pepper. Mix well to combine and rub or brush both sides of the ribs with the seasoning mix. Set aside for 30 minutes to absorb.
4. Place ribs with bone-side down in the air fryer basket. Place the basket back to the instant pot duo crisp and cover with the air fryer lid. Set to cook for 15 minutes at 375 degrees F. Flip over and cook for another 10 minutes.
5. Remove basket from the air fryer and brush ribs with the BBQ sauce.
6. Return the air fryer basket to the instant pot and cook for another 5 minutes or until desired crispness is achieved.

Nutritional Information (per 2 slices): Calories –441kcal; Carbohydrates – 26.8g; Fat – 29g; Protein – 18.2g; Sugar – 20g; Sodium – 1070mg;

Pork Meatballs

Preparation Time: 10 minutes
Cooking Time: 10 minutes
Yields: 12 servings

Ingredients

- 8 oz. ground Italian sausage, mild or hot
- 1 large egg
- ½ cup panko bread crumbs
- 12 oz. ground pork
- ½ tsp. dried paprika
- 1 tsp. dried parsley
- 1 tsp. salt

Directions

1. In a large bowl, combine bread crumbs, sausage, pork, egg, paprika, and parsley. Season with salt. Mix to thoroughly combine all ingredients.
2. Form into 12 meatballs of equal sizes, using an ice cream scoop. Place meatballs in an air fryer basket lined with parchment paper. You may use a two-layer of air fryer basket to accommodate all meatballs in a single batch.
3. Place the air fryer basket in the instant pot duo crisp and attach the air fryer lid. Set to 350 degrees F and cook for 8 minutes. Shake basket and cook for another 2 minutes. Transfer to a platter and serve.

Nutritional Information (as per slices): Calories –57kcal; Carbohydrates – 3.8; Fat – 8.1g; Protein –8.5g; Sodium – 391mg;

Chapter 6 Poultry

Instant Pot Turkey Breast

Preparation Time: 5 minutes
Cooking Time: 50 minutes
Yields: 8 servings

Ingredients

- 6½ lbs. bone-in and skin-on turkey breast
- 1 (14 oz.) can turkey broth or chicken broth
- 1 stalk celery, cut in large pieces
- 1 large onion, quartered
- 1 sprig thyme
- 3 tbsps. cornstarch
- 3 tbsps. cold water
- Salt and pepper to taste

Directions

1. Generously season the turkey breast with salt and pepper.
2. Set the trivet at the bottom of the inner steel pot of your cooker. Add the celery, onions, thyme, and broth. Place the turkey on the trivet with the breast-side up.
3. Close the cooker with the pressure cooker lid. Pressure cook on HIGH for about 30 minutes.
4. Once the cooking time ends, turn off the pressure cooker. Allow to release the pressure naturally for about 10 minutes then use the quick pressure release.
5. Once the valve drops, carefully remove the lid. Insert the meat thermometer in the thickest part of the breast to check if the turkey is already cooked. It should read 165 degrees F; continue to cook at High Pressure for a few more minutes if necessary.
6. Once done, use the trivet to remove the turkey from the cooker and transfer to a platter. Cover the turkey with foil and let it rest for a while.
7. Make the gravy by pouring the juices in the cooking pot through a strainer. Skim off the fat using a ladle or a fat separator.
8. Create slurry by combining the cornstarch and cold water. Stir into the broth in the cooking pot, then season with salt and pepper.
9. Now, if you don't plan to brown the turkey, discard the foil and remove the skin of the turkey. Slice the turkey and serve it immediately. On the other hand, if you like your turkey browned, transfer the gravy to a serving dish and wash the cooking pot. Bring the turkey (still set on the trivet) back to the pot and attach the air fryer lid to the instant pot. Air-fry at 350 degrees F for about 15 minutes or until browned. Constant monitoring is required if you want the turkey done to perfection.

Nutritional Information (as per serving): Calories – 122; Carbohydrates – 7g; Fat – 2g; Fiber – 0g; Protein – 19g; Sodium – 300mg; Sugar – 2g

Instant Pot Rotisserie Chicken

Preparation: 5 minutes
Cooking: 60 minutes
Yields: 4 servings

Ingredients

- 1 whole chicken, cleaned and patted dry
- 2 tbsps. olive oil
- 1 tbsp. seasoned salt

Directions

1. Make sure that the giblet packet from the chicken cavity is removed.
2. Rub the oil all over the chicken and generously season with salt.
3. Put the chicken with the breast-side down in your air fryer basket.
4. Cook for 30 minutes at 350 degrees F.
5. Once done, flip the chicken over and cook for another 30 minutes or until the internal temperature reads 165 degrees F.
6. Once cooked, let the chicken rest for about 10 minutes and serve.

Nutritional Information (as per serving): Calories – 464; Carbohydrates – 0g; Fat – 36g; Fiber – 0g; Protein – 35g; Sodium – 1877mg; Sugar – 0g

Asian Sticky Wings

Preparation: 5 minutes
Cooking: 40 minutes
Yields: 4 servings

Ingredients
- 1 lb. chicken wings
- 2 cups of water
- 1 tsp. sea salt, divided
- ¼ cup honey
- ½ cup rice vinegar
- 2 tsps. red chili pepper paste
- 2 cloves garlic, minced
- 1 tsp. ginger, freshly grated
- Zest and juice of 1 small orange
- A dash of chopped green onions, crushed peanuts, or chopped cilantro to serve

Directions
1. Add 2 cups of water to the inner steel pot and set the trivet in low position inside the pot.
2. Arrange the wings on the trivet and put the pressure lid on. Set the pressure on HIGH and cook it for 2 minutes. Once the time is up, release the pressure and remove the lid.
3. Meanwhile, combine the orange zest & juice, rice vinegar, honey, red pepper paste, ginger, garlic, and ½ teaspoon of salt in a bowl.
4. Carefully remove the chicken wings and the trivet from the pot. Put the wings on a tray lined with paper towels. Pat them dry, removing as much moisture as possible. Season them with the remaining teaspoon of salt.
5. Next, put the sauce in the inner pot of the instant pot and place the trivet in low position into the inner pot. Arrange the wings on the trivet in a single layer.
6. Air fry the wings at 390 degrees F for 30 minutes. Flip the wings every 10 minutes until your desired color is achieved.
7. Once done, remove the trivet and put the wings into the sauce. Stir everything to coat then remove from the pot to cool.
8. To serve, you can top with chopped green onions, crushed peanuts, or chopped cilantro.

Nutritional Information (as per serving): Calories – 431; Carbohydrates – 42g; Fat – 19g; Fiber – 1g; Protein – 23g; Sodium – 1256mg; Sugar – 39g

Crisp Greek Chicken & Potatoes

Preparation: 20 minutes
Cooking: 27-30 minutes
Yields: 6 servings

Ingredients

- 12 bone-in chicken thighs
- 1½ lbs. yellow potatoes
- ½ cup chicken broth
- ⅓ cup olive oil
- ⅓ cup lemon juice
- 1 tsp. lemon zest
- 1 tbsp. garlic, minced
- 2 tsps. dried oregano
- 1 tsp. dried parsley
- 1 tsp. black pepper
- 2 tsps. Kosher salt
- 2 lemon wedges, for garnish

Directions

1. Whisk the lemon juice, olive oil, garlic, parsley, oregano, pepper, lemon zest, and salt in a bowl.
2. If your potatoes are large, cut them into quarters; but if they're small, cut them into halves.
3. Add the chicken broth into your instant pot and arrange the chicken thighs in a single layer. Pour half of the lemon juice mixture over the chicken thighs.
4. Layer the potatoes on top of the thighs and pour the remaining half of the lemon juice mixture over the potatoes.
5. Pressure cook for 15 minutes, and once the time is up, let the pot sit for about 10 minutes. Make sure to move the valve for venting.
6. Once done, remove the lid and transfer the potatoes to a serving dish. Transfer the chicken to a platter and the juices to a container.
7. To brown the chicken, arrange the chicken thighs (in batches as needed) in the fryer basket. Set a tall trivet in the inner steel pot of your cooker and place the basket on top of it.
8. Place the air fryer lid, set the temperature to 500 degrees F and cook for 4 minutes.
9. Put the chicken together with the potatoes in the serving dish. To serve, pour in some of the reserved juices and garnish with lemon wedges.

Nutritional Information (as per 2 thighs): Calories – 679; Carbohydrates – 22g; Fat – 44.4g; Fiber – 2.9g; Protein – 47.8g; Sodium – 1239mg; Sugar – 1.4g

Chicken Fillet

Preparation: 5 minutes
Cooking: 25 minutes
Yields: 3 servings

Ingredients

- 3 chicken breast fillets
- ¾ cup chicken stock, divided
- 2 tbsps. olive oil, divided
- 1 tsp. Italian seasoning
- ½ tsp. ground coriander
- ½ tsp. paprika
- ½ tsp. garlic, minced
- ½ tsp. ground ginger
- Salt and pepper to taste

Directions

1. Mix the Italian seasoning, coriander, paprika, garlic, ginger, pepper, salt, 2 tablespoons chicken stock, and 1 tablespoon olive oil in a small bowl.
2. Put the chicken into a bowl and pour the paste to the chicken. Rub the breasts with the paste to coat completely.
3. Press the SAUTE setting of your instant pot and add the oil into the pot. Add the chicken breasts and cook for 2 minutes per side or until they're browned on both sides.
4. Transfer the chicken breasts to a plate and set aside.
5. Add the remaining chicken stock to the instant pot. Use a wooden or silicon spoon to scrape the fond at the bottom of the pot.
6. Set the trivet inside and arrange the chicken fillets on top of it.
7. Pressure cook on HIGH for 5 minutes.
8. Once done, let it naturally release the pressure for about 8-10 minutes before quick releasing.
9. Remove the chicken and the trivet from the pot; transfer the stock to a container.
10. Set the trivet in the inner pot again and place the chicken breasts on top.
11. Attach the air fryer lid to the instant pot and air-fry at 350 degrees F for 20 minutes, flipping the chicken halfway through the cooking process.
12. Transfer to a serving plate and serve with your favorite greens or side dish.

Nutritional Information *(as per chicken breast)*: Calories – 265; Carbohydrates – 2g; Fat – 13g; Fiber – 0g; Protein – 35g; Sodium – 202mg; Sugar – 0g

Honey-mustard Chicken Breasts

Preparation: 10 minutes
Cooking: 20 minutes
Yields: 6 chicken breasts

Ingredients

- 6 oz. boneless and skinless chicken breasts
- 2 tbsps. fresh rosemary, minced
- 3 tbsps. honey
- 1 tbsp. Dijon mustard
- ¼ tsp. ground black pepper
- ¾ tsp. salt

Directions

1. Combine the honey, Dijon mustard, black pepper, rosemary, and salt in a bowl.
2. Rub the chicken breasts with the honey-mustard mixture.
3. Spritz the air fryer basket generously with cooking spray. Arrange the chicken breasts inside the basket in a single layer (work in batches if necessary).
4. Place the trivet inside the pot and place the basket on top.
5. Air-fry at 350 degrees F for about 20-24 minutes or until the thermometer inserted at the center of the chicken reads 165 degrees F.
6. Transfer the chicken breasts to a platter. Serve with green veggies, rice, or quinoa.

Nutritional Information (as per chicken breast): Calories – 236; Carbohydrates – 9.8g; Fat – 5g; Fiber – 1g; Protein – 38g; Sodium – 759mg; Sugar – 8.8g

Chicken-Parmesan Wings

Preparation: 10 minutes
Cooking: 15 minutes
Yields: 4 servings

Ingredients
- 2 lbs. chicken wings, cut into drumettes and wingettes
- ½ cup + 6 tbsps. Parmesan, freshly grated
- 1 tsp. Herbs de Provence
- 1 tsp. paprika
- Salt to taste

Directions
1. Pat the chicken wings dry, put them in a bowl and set aside.
2. Combine the Parmesan, Herbs de Provence, paprika, and salt in a small bowl.
3. Coat the wings with the Parmesan mixture.
4. Preheat your instant pot with the air fryer lid on at 350 degrees F.
5. Spritz the air fryer basket with cooking spray. Arrange the wings in the basket in a single layer (work in batches as necessary).
6. Set the trivet inside the pot and place the basket on top of it.
7. Air-fry the chicken wings for 15 minutes, turning them halfway through.
8. Garnish the wings with extra Parmesan and fresh herbs before serving.

Nutritional Information (as per serving): Calories – 490; Carbohydrates – 1g; Fat – 22g; Fiber – 0g; Protein – 72g; Sodium – 639mg; Sugar – 0g

Chicken Tikka Kebab

Preparation: 4 minutes
Cooking: 15 minutes
Yields: 4 servings

Ingredients

- 1½ lbs. chicken breasts, pat dry
- 2 cups mixed peppers
- 1 medium red onion, sliced

For the marinade:

- ½ cup plain yogurt
- 2 tbsps. garlic paste
- 1 tbsp. oil
- ½ tbsp. lemon juice
- 2 tsps. cornstarch
- 1½ tsps. Kosher salt
- 1 tsp. green chili
- 1 tsp. ginger
- 1 tsp. ground white pepper

- ½ tsp. Garam masala

For the mint-cilantro chutney:

- ½ cup cilantro
- ¼ cup mint leaves
- 2 small green chilies
- 1 clove garlic
- 2 tbsps. unsweetened coconut
- 1 tbsp. lemon juice
- 1 tsp. sugar
- 1 tsp. Kosher salt
- ½ tsp. cumin seeds
- 2 tablespoons of water

Directions

1. Cut the chicken, mixed peppers, and red onion into 1½-inch slices.
2. Add all the marinade ingredients in a medium-size bowl and mix well. Add the chicken slices and mix well to coat. Marinate for at least 4 hours (preferably overnight) in the refrigerator.
3. Thread the chicken, peppers, and onion slices in the skewers. Spritz them with cooking spray.
4. Spritz the fryer basket with cooking spray and place the kebabs in it.
5. Place the tall trivet into the instant pot and put the basket on top of it.
6. Attach the air fryer lid to the instant pot and cook the kebabs at 400 degrees F for 15 minutes.
7. Meanwhile, make the chutney by processing everything in a blender with 2 tablespoons of water. You can add a bit of water if necessary.
8. Once the kebabs are cooked, transfer them to a platter or tray. Serve with the mint-cilantro chutney on the side.
9. Enjoy.

Nutritional Information (as per serving): Calories – 319; Carbohydrates – 16g; Fat – 11g; Fiber – 2g; Protein – 39g; Sodium – 1681mg; Sugar – 4g

Super Crispy Chicken Wings

Preparation: 5 minutes
Cooking: 40 minutes
Yields: 24 chicken wings

Ingredients
- 24 Party-style chicken wings
- 1 cup chicken broth
- ½ cup hot sauce
- ¼ cup butter
- 1 tbsp. white vinegar
- ¼ tsp. Worcestershire sauce
- ¼ tsp. cayenne pepper
- ⅛ tsp. garlic powder
- Seasoned salt to taste
- A pinch of celery for garnish
- A tablespoon ranch dressing or blue cheese, for dipping

Directions
1. Pour the broth into the instant pot and arrange the wings in the fryer basket.
2. Set the trivet in the instant pot and place the basket on top of it.
3. Pressure cook on HIGH for 10 minutes.
4. Meanwhile, add the butter, Worcestershire sauce, hot sauce, cayenne, garlic powder, salt, and vinegar in a small saucepan.
5. Place the saucepan over medium-high heat and whisk the ingredients until the butter melts and the mixture starts to bubble around the edges.
6. Turn off the heat and let the sauce stand while you prepare the wings.
7. Do a quick release and once done, remove the air fryer basket.
8. Discard the liquid in the pot or set aside in a container.
9. Generously spritz the wings with cooking spray and toss to coat thoroughly.
10. Place the trivet and the basket inside the instant pot.
11. Attach the air fryer lid to the instant pot and air fry at 400 degrees F for 20 minutes, tossing the wings every 5 minutes.
12. During the last 5 minutes of cooking the wings, reheat the sauce on low heat.
13. Once the wings are done, remove them from the pot. Transfer the wings to a plate or serving dish and coat them with sauce.
14. Garnish with celery and serve with ranch dressing or blue cheese on the side.

Nutritional Information (as per 4 wings): Calories – 464; Carbohydrates – 10g; Fat – 40g; Fiber – 1g; Protein – 16g; Sodium – 1647mg; Sugar – 1g

Mini Egg Bake

Preparation: 5 minutes
Cooking: 30 minutes
Yields: 6 servings

Ingredients

- 1 lb. ground turkey sausage
- 2 large eggs
- ½ cup of half-and-half
- ½ cup of cheddar cheese, shredded
- 1 small broccoli head, cut into florets
- 1 red bell pepper, diced
- 1 medium onion, chopped
- 2 cloves garlic, minced
- 1 tbsp. olive oil
- Salt and pepper to taste
- A dash of hot sauce to serve

Directions

1. Hit the SAUTE setting and add the oil. Once hot, sauté the sausage and let them brown for about 2-3 minutes.
2. Add the onions and garlic; sauté for another 2 minutes or until the onions are translucent.
3. Next, add the broccoli and red bell peppers. Cook for another 3-4 minutes, occasionally stirring until the broccoli florets are slightly tender.
4. Turn off the SAUTE mode and transfer the sausage-veggie mixture to a large plate.
5. Break the eggs in a large bowl. Add the half-and-half, salt, and pepper then whisk until the mixture is smooth.
6. Grease six 8-ounce ramekins. Add about a quarter cup of the sausage mixture into each ramekin and cover them with egg mixture. Sprinkle about 1½ tablespoons of shredded cheddar cheese on top of each ramekin.
7. Set the tall trivet inside the steel pot of your instant pot and place the fryer basket on top of it.
8. Put three ramekins in the basket (cook in two batches as needed).
9. Attach the air fryer lid and air fry at 320 degrees F for 10 minutes.
10. Repeat step 8 and 9 with the remaining ramekins. Garnish with green onions and drizzle with hot sauce before serving.

Nutritional Information (as per ramekin): Calories – 320; Carbohydrates – 7g; Fat – 20g; Fiber – 1g; Protein – 28g; Sodium – 709mg; Sugar – 3g

Cheesy Frittata

Preparation: 10 minutes
Cooking: 15- 22 minutes
Yields: 6 servings

Ingredients
- 4 large eggs
- 3 cups spinach
- ¾ cup onion, diced
- ⅓ cup tomatoes, diced
- ⅓ cup Cheddar cheese, shredded
- ⅓ cup feta cheese
- 1 tbsp. half-and-half
- ¾ tsp. Kosher salt
- ¼ tsp. ground black pepper
- 2 green onions, sliced

Directions
1. Break all the eggs in a bowl and whisk together with the half-and-half, salt, and pepper. Add the onions, spinach, tomatoes, feta cheese, and cheddar cheese, then mix well.
2. Spritz a 6-inch deep round pan with cooking spray. Pour the egg mixture into it.
3. Set the trivet in the inner pot of the instant pot and carefully place the round pan on top of it.
4. Put the air fryer lid on and air fry at 350 degrees F for about 15-22 minutes or until your desired doneness is achieved.
5. Once done, carefully take out the round pan. To serve, top the frittata with sliced green onions.

Nutritional Information (as per serving): Calories – 185; Carbohydrates – 8.5g; Fat – 11g; Fiber – 3g; Protein – 13g; Sodium – 540mg; Sugar – 3.3g

Southern-style Chicken

Preparation: 15 minutes
Cooking: 30 minutes
Yields: 6 servings

Ingredients

- 1 broiler or fryer chicken (about 4 lbs.), cut into pieces
- 2 cups bread crumbs
- 1 large egg, beaten
- 1 tbsp. fresh parsley, minced
- 1 tsp. garlic salt
- 1 tsp. paprika
- ½ tsp. pepper
- ¼ tsp. ground cumin
- ¼ tsp. sage, rubbed

Directions

1. Preheat your air fryer to 375 degrees F and spritz the fryer basket with cooking spray.
2. Mix the bread crumbs, parsley, garlic salt, paprika, pepper, ground cumin, and sage in a shallow bowl. Crack the egg in another bowl and whisk lightly.
3. Dip the chicken cuts into the whisked egg then into the cracker mixture. Pat for the coating to stick to the chicken.
4. Arrange the chicken pieces in a single layer in the basket and spritz the chicken with cooking spray.
5. Working in batches, air fry for 10 minutes, then flip the chicken. Spritz them with more cooking spray to make them crispier. Continue to cook for 10-20 minutes longer until golden brown and the juices run clear.
6. Serve warm.

Nutritional Information (as per serving): Calories – 403; Carbohydrates – 13g; Fat – 23g; Fiber – 1g; Protein – 36g; Sodium – 460mg; Sugar – 2g

Air-fried Breaded Chicken

Preparation: 10 minutes
Cooking: 15 minutes
Yields: 4 servings

Ingredients

- 6-oz. boneless and skinless chicken breasts
- ¼ cup bread crumbs
- ⅛ tsp. garlic powder
- ⅛ tsp. paprika
- ¼ tsp. oregano
- Salt and pepper to taste

Directions

1. Preheat your air fryer to 390 degrees F.
2. Mix the bread crumbs, garlic powder, paprika, salt, pepper and oregano in a medium bowl until well combined.
3. Spritz the chicken breasts with cooking spray then dredge them one by one into the breadcrumb mixture. Shake off any extra breading and arrange them in the air fryer basket. Make sure to assemble them in a single layer, not over-crowding them. Work in batches if needed.
4. Generously spritz the breaded chicken with cooking spray to help them crisp up.
5. Air fry at 350 degrees F for 5 minutes. Flip the chicken and spritz some cooking spray on them. Continue to cook for additional 4-7 minutes or until they're golden brown. Remember, cooking time will depend on the thickness and size of the chicken breasts.
6. Serve and enjoy.

Nutritional Information (as per breaded chicken): Calories – 204; Carbohydrates – 5g; Fat – 4g; Fiber – 0g; Protein – 37g; Sodium – 246mg; Sugar – 0.5g

Crispy Chicken-vegetable Rolls

Preparation Time: 15 minutes
Cooking Time: 50 minutes
Yields: 6 servings

Ingredients

- 2 tbsps. vegetable oil
- 1 lb. ground chicken
- 3 cloves garlic, minced
- 1 tbsp. soy sauce
- 1 large egg
- 1 package egg roll wrappers or Spring roll pastry
- Olive oil or oil spray for coating
- ½ tsp. salt to taste
- ½ tsp. sesame seed oil
- Freshly grated black pepper to taste
- ½ cup carrot, grated
- 2 cups cabbage, sliced thinly
- 3 green onions, chopped
- 1 tsp. freshly grated ginger root, optional

For Hoisin-Peanut Dip:

- ½ tsp chili hot sauce or Sriracha sauce, optional
- ½ tsp. sesame oil to taste
- ¼ cup peanut butter
- ½ cup hoisin sauce
- 2 tsps. vinegar
- ½ cup water

Directions

1. To make egg roll filling, add garlic and ginger (optional) to the inner pot of the instant pot duo crisp. Cover with the pressure cooker lid and set to sauté function. Cook for about a minute or until lightly brown.
2. Add the ground chicken along with the sesame seed oil, season with soy sauce, salt, and pepper to taste. Cook for 1-2 minutes until chicken turns slightly brown and tender.
3. Add in green onions, cabbage, and carrots and cook for another 1-2 minutes until vegetables soften but still crisp.
4. Stir in the egg and continue cooking for another 30 minutes.
5. Remove from heat, strain to drain excess juice. Leave to cool.
6. To make the Hoisin-Peanut dip, combine peanut butter, sesame oil, hot sauce, rice vinegar, and water in a bowl. Whisk altogether. You may use a blender to blend all ingredients. Note that some hoisin brands are very thick that you need more water.
7. Lay egg roll wrapper on a flat surface and add 1 tablespoon or 2 of the chicken filling. Tuck and roll tightly.
8. Seal edges using beaten eggs or water. Repeat the process until all fillings are used up.
9. Spray each chicken roll with oil and arrange them inside the air fryer basket.
10. Dislodge the pressure cooker lid from the instant pot and replace with the air fryer lid.
11. Air fry at 380 degrees F for 15 minutes, flipping halfway through for even cooking until they become crispy and light brown.
12. Serve immediately while warm with the hoisin-peanut dip.

Nutritional Information (as per serving): Calories – 808 kcal; Fat – 23.59g; Carbohydrates – 130.32g; Protein – 18.82 g; sugar – 18.97g; Fiber – 3.6g; Sodium – 877 mg

Air Fryer Bacon Wrapped Hot Dogs

Preparation Time: 5 minutes
Cooking Time: 15 minutes
Yields: 4 servings
Ingredients
- 4 hot dogs
- 4 slices of bacon
- 4 hot dog buns
- For serving: mustards, ketchup, pickles, jalapenos, onions, and BBQ sauce

Directions
1. Wrap hot dogs with bacon slices, making sure that they cover the tips of the hot dogs. Arrange in a single layer inside the instant pot duo crisp air fryer basket.
2. Snugly wrap bacon slices around hot dogs and make sure that it covers the tips. Place hot dogs in the air fryer basket.
3. Insert the air fryer basket to the instant pot and attach the air fryer lid.
4. Air-fry at 380 degrees F for 8-10 minutes. If you want your hot dogs with bacon extra crispy, cook at 400 degrees F and adjust cooking time to 6-8 minutes.
5. Serve bacon-wrapped hot dogs in the buns and then air-fry for a minute to keep bread crispy.
6. Insert bacon-wrapped hot dogs in the hot dog buns and air-fry for another minute or until the bread is warm. Serve with your favorite toppings.

Nutritional Information (as per serving): Calories – 141 kcal; Carbohydrates – 21.12 g; Fat – 4.13 g; Protein – 4.96 g; Fiber - 0.09 g; Sugar – 2.73 g; Sodium – 241 mg

Fryer Chicken Wings

Preparation Time: 10 minutes
Cooking Time: 30 minutes
Yields: 4 servings

Ingredients

- 2 lbs. chicken wings
- Black pepper and Kosher salt to taste
- Optional: garlic salt to taste

Directions

1. Cleanse and pat dry chicken wings.
2. Season with salt and pepper to taste.
3. Add garlic salt if desired but this is optional.
4. Place them in the instant pot air fryer basket. Attach air fryer lid and set to air frying. Cook at 400 degrees F for 30-35 minutes, flipping about three times for even cooking.
5. Serve with desired sauce for a dip.

Nutritional Information (as per serving): Calories – 277 kcal; Carbohydrates – 1.06g; Fat – 8.05 g; Protein – 50.05 g; Fiber - 1.6 g; Sugar – 0.57 g; Sodium – 184 mg

Air Fryer Baked Egg Cups Spinach & Cheese

Preparation Time: 5 minutes
Cooking Time: 10 minutes
Yields: 1 serving
Ingredients
- 1-2 tsps. grated cheese
- 1 large egg
- 1 tbsp. frozen spinach, thawed and sautéed
- 1 tbsp. milk or half-and-half
- Salt and ground pepper to taste
- Cooking spray

Directions
1. Prepare the ramekins by spraying it with cooking spray.
2. Add all ingredients into the ramekins and add salt and pepper to season.
3. Lightly stir to avoid breaking the egg yolk.
4. Place ramekins inside the air fryer basket and into the instant pot. Attach the air fryer lid and set to Baking. Cook at 330 degrees F for 6-12 minutes. You may cook in batches if preparing more cups.
5. Serve and enjoy.

Nutritional Information (as per serving): Calories – 130 kcal; Carbohydrates – 10.93 g; Fat – 6.6 g; Protein – 6.6 g; Fiber - 1.6 g; Sugar – 6.08 g; Sodium – 152 mg

Chapter 7 Desserts

Air Fryer Brownies

Preparation Time: 5 minutes
Cooking Time: 18 minutes
Yields: 2 servings
Ingredients
- 1 large egg
- ½ cup of granulated sugar
- ¼ cup all-purpose flour
- ⅓ cup cocoa powder
- ¼ tsp. baking soda
- ¼ cup butter, melted
- A pinch of salt

Directions
1. Prepare a 6-inch Spring form pan and grease with cooking spray.
2. In a medium-size mixing bowl, add sugar, flour, cocoa powder, salt, and baking powder. Mix thoroughly all ingredients to combine.
3. In another bowl, whisk egg and butter until fully blended. Then add wet ingredients to dry ingredients and stir until completely mixed.
4. Transfer the batter to the baking pan and smoothen the top to flatten evenly. Place the pan inside the pot over a trivet and cook at 350 degrees F for 16-18 minutes.
5. Once done, allow to cool and slice to serve.

Nutritional Information (as per serving): Calories – 451 kcal; Carbohydrates – 45.49 g; Fat – 27.23g; Protein – 5.78 g; Sugar – 24.81g; Sodium – 354mg

Air-Fried Cinnamon Rolls

Preparation Time: 5 minutes
Cooking Time: 10 minutes
Yields: 6 servings
Ingredients
For the Rolls
- ⅓ cup packed brown sugar
- 2 tbsps. melted butter (+ more for brushing)
- ½ tsp. ground cinnamon
- Kosher salt to taste
- 8-oz. crescent rolls, tube-refrigerated
- All-purpose flour for surface

For the Glaze
- 1 tbsp. whole milk (+ more if needed)
- 2 oz. cream cheese, softened
- ½ cup powdered sugar

Directions
1. To make rolls, prepare by lining air fryer basket with parchment paper. Grease with butter.
2. Add butter, cinnamon, brown sugar, and a pinch of salt. Mix thoroughly the ingredients until it turns smooth and fluffy.
3. Sprinkle flour lightly over a flat surface and roll out crescent rolls in one piece. Fold in half and pinch seams together before rolling it to form a 9x7-inch rectangle.
4. Spread butter mixture over it, keeping a 1/4 -inch border on all sides. Roll the dough up starting from its long edge and cut crosswise into six pieces.
5. Arrange rolls inside the air fryer basket, space evenly with cut-side up.
6. Place the air fryer basket inside the instant pot and attach the air fryer lid. Set the timer to 10 minutes and cook at 350 degrees F.
7. To make the glaze, whisk milk and powdered sugar with cream cheese in a mixing bowl. If necessary, you may add more milk by a teaspoonful to thin glaze.
8. Spread glaze over warm cinnamon before serving fresh from the air fryer.

Nutritional Information (as per serving): Calories – 229 kcal; Carbohydrates – 31.84 g; Fat – 9.25 g; Protein – 4.49 g; Fiber - 0.9 g; Sugar – 22.24 g; Sodium – 229 mg

Chocolate Smarties Cookies

Preparation Time: 5 minutes
Cooking Time: 8 minutes
Yields: 8 servings
Ingredients:
- 3.5 oz. butter
- 3.5 oz. caster sugar
- 7.5 oz. self-raising flour
- 1 tsp. vanilla essence
- 1 tbsp. milk
- 3 tbsps. cocoa powder
- 2 oz. Smarties

Directions
1. In a large mixing bowl, combine self-rising flour with cocoa powder.
2. Using your hands, mix butter and flour thoroughly until it forms into coarse bread crumbs.
3. Add in milk and vanilla essence and mix to blend.
4. Gradually add the Smarties and start kneading the cookie dough until it becomes soft and forms into a ball.
5. Serve.

Nutritional Information (as per serving): Calories – 239 kcal; Carbohydrates – 31.89 g; Fat – 10.77 g; Protein – 3.7 g; Fiber - 1.9 g; Sugar – 4.21 g; Sodium – 86 mg

Lava Molten Cake

Preparation Time: 5 minutes
Cooking Time: 13 minutes
Yields: 4 servings

Ingredients
- 2 eggs
- 1½ tbsps. self-rising flour
- 3.5 oz. unsalted butter
- 3½ tbsps. baker's sugar, not powdered
- 3.5 oz. dark chocolate, cut into pieces or chopped
- A drizzle of raspberries to serve

Directions
1. Prepare 4 safe-oven ramekins. Grease them with butter or cooking spray.
2. Melt butter and dark chocolates for 3 minutes, level 7 on your microwave. Remove from heat before it is totally melted and stir thoroughly, allowing remaining heat from butter and chocolate to completely melt the mixture.
3. Beat or whisk eggs and sugar in a mixing bowl until frothy and pour over the chocolate mixture into the egg mixture. Add in flour to combine thoroughly using a spatula.
4. Fill each ramekin (about 3/4 full) with the cake mixture. Place over the trivet inside the instant pot and cover with the air fryer lid attachment. Set to 375 degrees F and cook for 10 minutes.
5. Remove ramekins from the air fryer basket and allow to cool for about 2 minutes. Loosen edges with a knife and carefully turnover ramekin content into a serving plate while tapping its bottom.
6. Serve with a drizzle of raspberries.

Nutritional Information (as per serving): Calories – 392 kcal; Carbohydrates – 25.09 g; Fat – 29.08 g; Protein – 7.52 g; Fiber - 2.8 g; Sugar – 17.24 g; Sodium – 203 mg

Air-fried Donuts

Preparation Time: 2 hours
Cooking Time: 10 minutes
Yields: 8 servings

Ingredients

- 2 cups all-purpose flour
- ¼ cup warm water, 100-110 degrees F
- ¼ cup whole milk at room temperature
- 1 tsp. active dry yeast
- ¼ tsp. salt
- ¼ cup granulated sugar
- 2 tbsps. unsalted butter, melted
- 1 cup powdered sugar
- 1 large egg, beaten
- 4 tsps. tap water

Directions

1. In a small bowl, add the yeast, water, and half a teaspoon of the granulated sugar. Stir well to combine and let it stand for about 5 minutes until it becomes foamy.
2. In a medium-size mixing bowl, combine flour, salt and the remaining granulated sugar. Add the yeast mixture along with butter, milk, and egg. Stir the mixture using a wooden spoon until it forms into a soft dough and no longer sticks to the sides of the bowl.
3. Place dough on a lightly floured surface and knead until it becomes smooth, about 1-2 minutes.
4. Transfer the dough to a lightly greased bowl and cover with a plastic wrap. Allow the dough to rise until doubles in volume, about an hour.
5. As soon as the dough becomes double in size, transfer to a lightly floured surface. Roll it to about 1/4-inch in thickness.
6. Using a 3-inch round cutter, cut into 8 doughnuts. Use a 1-inch cutter for the hole at the center.
7. Make sure that the area where you place the doughnuts and doughnut holes is lightly floured to avoid doughnuts sticking to each other. Cover with plastic wrap and allow standing until doubles in size, about 30 minutes.
8. Place 2 doughnuts and 2 doughnut holes in the air fryer basket and place inside the instant pot duo crisp. Attach the air fryer lid and cook at 350 degrees F until golden brown. Repeat the process with the remaining doughnuts and doughnut holes.
9. To make the glaze, add powdered sugar and tap water in a medium bowl and whisk them together until smooth. Dip each doughnut and doughnut holes in the glaze before placing them on a wire rack to drip off. Allow cooling for the glaze to harden (about 10 minutes) before serving.

Nutritional Information (as per serving): Calories – 240 kcal; Carbohydrates – 46 g; Fat – 4g; Protein – 5g; Sugar – 22g; Sodium – 74mg

Key Lime Cheesecake

Preparation Time: 20 minutes
Cooking Time: 65 minutes
Yields: 8 servings

Ingredients

- 1 tbsp. butter, melted
- 1½ cups Graham cracker crumbs
- 24 oz. cream cheese, softened
- 1 tbsp. cornstarch
- 1 cup white sugar
- 3 large eggs
- 2 cups key lime juice
- 1 tbsp. lime zest, grated

Directions

1. Combine Graham cracker crumbs with butter and press the mix into the bottom of the air fryer basket lined with parchment paper. Refrigerate.
2. Add the cream cheese, lime peel, sugar, and cornstarch in a large mixing bowl. Using an immersion blender, blend the ingredients until smooth and fluffy. Gradually add in eggs while continuously beating to blend until smooth. Also, add key lime juice with a mixer on low mode. Finish mixing with your hand. Avoid over blending lest your cake will crack when baked.
3. Pour batter over the prepared base.
4. Place the basket inside the instant pot duo unit and use the air fryer lid to cover. Secure and set to bake at 300 degrees F for 65 minutes. Allow to cool and refrigerate overnight.

Nutritional Information (as per serving): Calories – 360 kcal; Carbohydrates – 9.84 g; Fat – 32.1 g; Protein –8.04 g; Fiber - 0.8 g; Sugar – 6.27 g; Sodium – 397 mg

Chocolate Chip Cookie

Preparation Time: 10 minutes
Cooking Time: 10 minutes
Yields: 2 mini cheesecakes

Ingredients

- 2 large eggs
- 16 oz. cream cheese, softened at room temperature
- ½ tsp. lemon juice
- 2 tbsps. sour cream
- 1 tsp. vanilla extract
- ¾ cup zero-calorie sweetener

Directions

1. Add eggs, vanilla, sweetener and lemon juice in a blender. Process until smooth and add the sour cream along with the cheese. Continue to free until silky and free of lumps. The creamier, the better.
2. Line the air fryer basket with parchment paper and pour the batter into it. Place inside the instant pot and cover with the air fryer lid.
3. Bake for 8-10 minutes at 350 degrees F.
4. Allow to cool in a wire rack and leave in the fridge overnight or at least 2-3 hours.

Nutritional Information (as per serving): Calories – 752 kcal; Carbohydrates – 9.87 g; Fat – 70.65 g; Protein – 19.22 g; Fiber - 0 g; Sugar – 38.36 g; Sodium – 1020 mg

Air Fried Chocolate Chips

Preparation Time: 15 minutes
Cooking Time: 12 minutes
Yields: 8 servings

Ingredients
- 1 cup chocolate chips or chunks
- ½ tsp. baking soda
- ½ cup butter, softened
- 1 egg
- 1 tsp. vanilla
- ½ cup light brown sugar
- 1½ cups all-purpose flour
- ¼ tsp. salt
- A scoop of vanilla ice cream to serve

Directions
1. Line 2 layers of the air fryer basket with parchment paper.
2. Cream altogether the butter and brown sugar. Then add the egg and vanilla along with the baking soda, flour, and salt. Stir in chocolate chunks.
3. Press cookie dough into the bottom of the air fryer. Attach the air fryer lid and bake for 10-12 minutes until edges are lightly browned.
4. Top with a scoop of vanilla ice cream to serve.

Nutritional Information (as per serving): Calories – 286 kcal; Carbohydrates – 24.79 g; Fat – 18.64 g; Protein – 4.82 g; Fiber - 2 g; Sugar – 3.52 g; Sodium – 262 mg

Chapter 8 Snacks

Air Fried Cheeseburgers

Preparation Time: 10 minutes
Cooking Time: 8 minutes
Yields: 4 servings

Ingredients
- 4 hamburger buns
- 1 lb. ground beef
- 1 tbsp. low-sodium soy sauce
- 2 cloves garlic, minced
- 4 slices American cheese
- Freshly ground black pepper to taste
- 1 red onion, thinly sliced
- 4 lettuce
- 4 teaspoons mayonnaise
- 4 sliced tomatoes
- Kosher salt to taste

Directions
1. Combine Beef with soy sauce, salt, pepper and garlic in a large mixing bowl. Mix thoroughly so the mixture can seep through the beef.
2. Shape marinated ground beef into patties and arrange in a single layer in the air fryer basket. If there's not enough space to accommodate all patties, cook in batches.
3. Put the air fryer basket on top of the metal trivet inside the instant pot.
4. Attach the air fryer lid and cook at 375 degrees F for about 4 minutes. Turn over for even cooking and cook for another 4 minutes.
5. Once done, remove the burgers quickly and top every burger with a slice of cheese.
6. Cook the remaining patties using the same procedure.
7. Spread mayo on hamburger buns and then arrange its filling using lettuce as the base followed by a burger with cheese, tomatoes, and onions on top.
8. Serve immediately while warm.

Nutritional Information (as per serving): Calories 745 – kcal; Carbohydrates – 41.55 g; Fat – 41.24 g; Protein – 52.09 g; Sugar – 11.22 g; Sodium – 1327 mg

Air-fried Pickles

Preparation Time: 10 minutes
Cooking Time: 10 minutes
Yields: 3 servings

Ingredients
- ¼ cup Parmesan, freshly grated
- 1 tsp. garlic powder
- 2 cups dill pickle slices
- ½ cup bread crumbs
- 1 large egg, whisked with a tablespoon of water
- 1 tsp. dried oregano
- A dash of ranch for dipping

Directions
1. Pat pickle chips dry using paper towels.
2. In a medium-size mixing bowl, add Parmesan, bread crumbs, garlic powder, and oregano. Stir to mix.
3. One by one, dredge pickle chips in egg and then in the breadcrumb mixture.
4. Work in batches to avoid overcrowding in the air fryer basket. Arrange chips in a single layer. Place air fryer basket inside the instant pot and attach the air fryer lid. Cook at 400 degrees F for 10 minutes.
5. Serve while warm with ranch for the dip.

Nutritional Information (as per serving): Calories – 45 kcal; Carbohydrates –6.85 g; Fat – 2.07 g; Protein – 4.31 g; Fiber - 0.4g; Sugar – 0.55 g; Sodium – 146 mg

Crispy Potatoes

Preparation Time: 10 minutes
Cooking Time: 20 minutes
Yields: 4 servings

Ingredients

- 1 tbsp. extra-virgin olive oil
- 1 lb. of baby potatoes, halved
- 1 tsp. garlic powder
- 1 tsp. Cajun seasoning, optional
- 1 tsp. Italian seasoning
- 1 tbsp. freshly chopped parsley, for garnish
- Freshly ground black pepper and salt to taste
- 1 lemon, juiced

Directions

1. Toss potatoes in oil in a large bowl with garlic powder, Cajun and Italian seasonings. Add salt and pepper to taste.
2. Place potatoes in the air fryer basket of your instant pot duo crisp and attach the air fryer lid. Cook for 10 minutes at 400 degrees F. Shake the air fryer basket to stir potatoes and cook for another 10 minutes until golden brown.
3. Remove from the instant pot and serve on a plate.
4. Squeeze lemon juice over potatoes and garnish with parsley to serve.

Nutritional Information (as per serving): Calories – 275 kcal; Carbohydrates –22.17 g; Fat – 1.73 g; Protein – 2.94 g; Fiber - 3.3 g; Sugar – 1.19 g; Sodium – 150 mg

Crispy Avocado Fries

Preparation Time: 15 minutes
Cooking Time: 8 minutes
Yields: 4 servings

Ingredients

- 2 large eggs
- 1.2 cups all-purpose flour
- 1 tbsp. water
- 2 avocados, cut into 8 wedges
- 1½ tsps. black pepper
- ½ cup panko bread crumbs
- 1 tsp. canola mayonnaise
- ½ cup no-salt added ketchup
- 1 tbsp. Sriracha chili sauce
- 1 tbsp. apple cider vinegar
- Cooking spray
- Salt to taste

Directions

1. Add flour and pepper in a shallow dish and stir to combine.
2. Lightly beat eggs with water in a bowl. Place the panko bread crumbs in another dish.
3. Dredge each avocado wedge first in the flour mixture and shaking off any excess coating. Then dip in the egg mixture, allowing to drip off before finally coating with the panko bread crumbs. Spray each wedge with the cooking spray.
4. Place wedges on the air fryer basket lined with parchment paper. Place the basket inside the instant pot and cover with the air fryer lid.
5. Cook at 400 degrees F and for 7-8 minutes, flipping halfway through for even cooking. Once done, remove wedges from the air fryer, transfer into a platter, and sprinkle with salt.
6. Meanwhile, prepare the dip by whisking together mayonnaise, vinegar, Sriracha, and ketchup in a mixing bowl.
7. Serve the avocado wedges with this dip.

Nutritional Information (as per serving): Calories – 266 kcal; Carbohydrates – 23g; Fat – 18g; Protein – 4g; Sugar – 5g; Sodium – 306mg

Air Fryer Zucchini Chips

Preparation Time: 10 minutes
Cooking Time: 12 minutes
Yields: 4 servings

Ingredients

- 1 large egg, beaten
- 1 cup panko bread crumbs
- 1 medium zucchini, thinly sliced
- ¾ cup Parmesan cheese, grated
- Cooking spray

Directions

1. Combine Parmesan cheese and panko bread crumbs in a shallow dish.
2. Break egg in a shallow dish or bowl and whisk.
3. Dip zucchini slices in the egg, one at a time and then dip into bread crumbs to coat. Lightly spray the coated slices of zucchini with cooking spray and arrange them in the air fryer basket lined with parchment paper.
4. Insert the air fryer basket into the instant pot duo crisp and attach the air fryer lid to cover. Attach the air fryer lid and air-fry at 350 degrees F for 10 minutes.
5. Remove from the air fryer, flip for even cooking and cook for another 2 minutes.

Nutritional Information (as per serving): Calories – 186 kcal; Carbohydrates – 21.1 g; Fat – 6.6 g; Protein – 10.8 g; Sugar –0.1 g; Sodium – 384 mg

Air Fryer Sweet Potato French Fries

Preparation Time: 10 minutes
Cooking Time: 24 minutes
Yields: 4 servings
Ingredients
- 1 lb. sweet potatoes, cut into ¼-inch French fry size
- ¼ tsp. garlic powder
- 1 tablespoon olive oil
- Salt to taste
- Optional: ground black pepper to taste

Directions
1. Cleanse sweet potatoes and pat dry.
2. Put sweet potatoes in a bowl, coating them with cooking oil and garlic powder.
3. Season with salt and pepper. Gently toss to blend ingredients and for even coating.
4. Arrange potato pieces in the instant pot duo crisp air fryer basket. Cover with the air fryer lid and set to air frying for 18-22 minutes at 380 degrees F. Shake basket halfway through for even cooking. Be careful not to break the pieces of sweet potatoes. Cook for another 2-4 minutes depending on desired crispiness.
5. Serve and enjoy.

Nutritional Information (as per serving): Calories – 203 kcal; Fat – 3.48g; Carbohydrates – 19.96 g; Protein – 2.32 g; Sugar – 0.89 g; Fiber – 2.5 g; Sodium – 46 mg

Air-fried Kale Chips

Preparation Time: 10 minutes
Cooking Time: 5 minutes
Yields: 2-4 servings

Ingredients

- 2 tbsps. olive oil
- 1 bunch of Tuscan kale, stems removed and leaves cut into 2-inch pieces
- ½ tsp. ground pepper
- ½ tsp. Kosher salt

Directions

1. Toss altogether olive oil, kale leaves, salt and pepper.
2. Place kale in the air fryer basket and insert into the instant pot duo crisp. Attach the air fryer lid to cover and air fry for about 5 minutes at 390 degrees F, shaking air fryer basket halfway through cooking.
3. Once done, transfer chips to a platter, taste and adjust seasonings.
4. Serve warm.

Nutritional Information (as per serving): Calories – 74 kcal; Carbohydrates – 2 g; Fat – 6.92 g; Protein – 0.83 g; Fiber - 0.07 g; Sugar – 0.67 g; Sodium – 298 mg

Air-fried Toasted Sticks

Preparation Time: 5 minutes
Cooking Time: 8 minutes
Yield: 6 servings

Ingredients
- ⅓ cup heavy cream
- 2 large eggs
- ⅓ cup whole milk
- ¼ tsp. ground cinnamon
- 1 tsp. maple syrup
- 3 tbsps. granulated sugar
- 6 thick pullman slices, cut into 3 parts (alternative: brioche or white loaf)
- ½ tsp. pure vanilla extract
- Kosher salt to taste

Directions
1. Beat eggs and add sugar, milk, cream, vanilla, cinnamon with salt in a large shallow baking dish. Coat bread with the mixture, turning for even coating at all sides.
2. Line air fryer basket with parchment paper before arranging French toasts sticks inside. Avoid overcrowding and work in batches when necessary.
3. Place the basket inside the instant pot, attach the air fryer lid to the pressure cooker and set to cook at 370 degrees F for 8 minutes, tossing halfway through for even cooking.
4. Drizzle maple syrup over toast and serve warm.

Nutritional Information (as per serving): Calories – 132 kcal; Carbohydrates – 18.37 g; Fat – 5.03 g; Protein – 3.21 g; Sugar – 7.05 g; Sodium – 110 mg

Air Fryer Banana Bread

Preparation Time: 10 minutes
Cooking Time: 35 minutes
Yields: 8 servings

Ingredients
- 2 medium ripe bananas, mashed
- ½ cup granulated sugar
- 2 large eggs, lightly beaten
- ⅓ cup plain nonfat yogurt
- 3/4 cup white whole wheat flour
- ¼ tsp. baking soda
- 1 tsp. cinnamon
- ½ tsp. Kosher salt
- 2 tbsps. vegetable oil
- 2 tsps. toasted walnuts, roughly chopped
- 1 tsp. vanilla extract
- Cooking spray

Directions
1. Line with parchment a 6-inch round cake pan and grease with cooking spray.
2. In a medium-size mixing bowl, add flour, baking soda, cinnamon, and salt. Set aside.
3. In another bowl, add eggs, mashed bananas, yogurt, oil, sugar, and vanilla, and whisk to blend. Slowly pour wet ingredients into the flour mixture and continue stirring to completely combine all ingredients.
4. Pour batter into the pan and sprinkle walnuts over it.
5. Insert a trivet into your instant pot and put the pan on top of it. Attach the air fryer lid and cook at 310 degrees F for about 30-35 minutes.
6. Once done, remove the pan with the bread and transfer to a wire rack to cool for about 15 minutes.
7. Transfer the bread to a platter and slice to serve.

Nutritional Information (as per serving): Calories – 186kcal; Carbohydrates – 29g; Fat –6 g; Protein – 4g; Sugar – 17g; Sodium – 184mg

Brussels Sprout Pizza

Preparation Time: 10 minutes
Cooking Time: 25 minutes
Yields: 4 servings

Ingredients

- 9 slices of pancetta
- 2 tsps. extra-virgin olive oil
- 2 cloves of garlic, minced
- Brussels sprouts, trimmed and thinly sliced
- 1½-inch pizza crust
- ½ tsp. fennel seed
- ½ tbsp. cheese

Directions

1. Place 1 teaspoon of olive oil in the inner pot with pancetta and set to Sauté mode for 5 minutes. Transfer pancetta to a plate lined with a paper towel.
2. Pour the remaining oil and sauté garlic until fragrant for about 20 seconds and add the sprouts. Continue cooking for 5-10 minutes more until the sprouts turn brown. Transfer sprouts with garlic to a bowl and add pancetta to the mixture. Add cheese and fennel seed to the bowl of sprouts and toss to coat.
3. Line air fryer with parchment paper and place pizza crust at the bottom. Spread the Brussels sprout mixture to fill in the crust.
4. Place the air fryer to the instant pot duo crust and attach the air fryer lid.
5. Bake at 450 degrees F for 10-15 minutes or until cheese is melted.
6. Slice to serve.

Nutritional Information (as per serving): Calories –513 kcal; Carbohydrates – 38.8g; Fat – 27.2 g; Protein – 28.6g; Sodium – 1309 mg

CPSIA information can be obtained
at www.ICGtesting.com
Printed in the USA
LVHW020504121220
674004LV00009B/227